MW00940742

Remembering **Colonel**

Remembering

Colonel

A Remarkable Therapy Dog

Skip Daynes

S KIP DAYNES worked on a ranch when he was young. This experience helped Skip learn the language of dogs and horses.

Skip's real name is Gerald, the same as his father. Skip's father also loved dogs. His grandfather, Royal Daynes, gave him the nickname because he could skip rocks in the water when he was six years old. Skip's great grandfather, John, came across the plains with the Mormon pioneers in 1862. John's oldest son, Joseph, was appointed by Brigham Young as the first organist in the Tabernacle on Temple Square in Salt Lake City at the age of 13. He played for 33 years after helping install the organ.

The family business, Daynes Music, started in 1862 and became a Steinway piano dealer in 1873. It is now the oldest retail store in Utah and oldest Steinway dealer west of New York. Skip has been President for 44 years and is now 74 years old. He is at work every day and still moves pianos.

Colonel and Skip took an entire year to write this book. Colonel sat by his master in his home office checking out the details of his own story. Often Skip had to change things that just didn't' seem acceptable to Colonel. Susan, Skip's wife, took Colonel to the hospitals and was also very helpful with the book. This is a story about a smart and perceptive therapy dog that loved his work and made a great impact wherever he went.

Remembering Colonel
A Remarkable Therapy Dog

© 2013 by **Skip Daynes**. All rights reserved.

No part of this book may be reproduced in any written, electronic, recording, or photocopying without written permission of the publisher or author. The exception would be in the case of brief quotations embodied in the critical articles or reviews and pages where permission is specifically granted by the publisher or author.

Although every precaution has been taken to verify the accuracy of the information contained herein, the author and publisher assume no responsibility for any errors or omissions. No liability is assumed for damages that may result from the use of information contained within.

Interior and Cover design by Jimmy Sevilleno.

ISBN-13: 978-1491237915
ISBN-10: 1491237910

Table of Contents

Introduction

*M*OST OF US love our animals and feel happy when we are around them. We can watch their eyes stare at us for long periods of time. They are saying, "I love you, what can I do to show my love?"

Colonel has a psychic perception of what humans need. I have had many dogs and other pets and none have had intuition to his level. He is truly a unique dog. Most people who knew Colonel called him "special boy." This memoir is his story, in his words, written by his loving master.

In 1989, our youngest son Tim was invited by his best friend Ryan to go to Lake Powell, Utah. It was to be the best trip ever: the family had rented a houseboat. Their water-ski boat was new and one of the best. After cliff diving and skiing, they parked the houseboat near Halls Crossing. A burst of wind came up and blew a rubber raft from the top of the boat.

Tim was elected to swim out and retrieve the raft. He ran through the water until it was up above his calves and then did a racing-style dive—head first into a sand bar. With the wind blowing up waves, he had not seen the sand, pushed up by the houseboat, rising out farther in the lake. Tim was under the water for what seemed forever until someone finally pulled him out. He had shattered his C2, C3, and C4 vertebrae, and was paralyzed.

We received the call that Tim would be flown up to the University Medical Center by helicopter. Tim arrived the 28th of June, 1989, and was rushed into surgery, where a metal plate was placed in his neck. None of his lost function came back. He now needed to come to grips with the fact that he was a quadriplegic and, some said, "would never walk again."

Six and one half months later he finally left University Hospital after much hope and lots of work. He rolled out in his wheelchair to our home with several flights of stairs. After lots of hurdles and some luck, Tim received Yazanoff II (Yaz), a Golden Retriever/Yellow-Lab mix. This marvelous dog changed his, and our, lives forever.

We now speak dog language, live in a dog house, and raise puppies that have touched hundreds of lives in their daily service to others. The Daynes family has loved, trained and lived with Dutchie, Florabell (Flora), Alba, Colonel, Tanny, Devi, and now Reginald (Reggie). We deeply thank our dear friends at Canine Companions for Independence (CCI), Southwest Region, Oceanside, California for the opportunity to work with these marvelous animals.

Dogs think and understand third grade English. (So says Dean Koontz in his book about his own dog in *A Big Little Life*.) Golden Retrievers are the most interesting dogs because of their intense love for their masters. It is very deep and sincere. Often Golden lovers, like me, are a little weird. We think that we can understand their thoughts. I not only think, but also know, that most of the words in this story are his.

The setting for the start of this story is Hemet, California, on Cathy's ranch. Cathy Phillips is known by CCI as one of the great puppy producers. Her female Golden, JoLee, was legendary and produced many wonderful puppies that went on to fame. Colonel was one of Cathy's favorites, and this story is his story, in his words. His words become more intelligent as he gets older. You will notice his improved ability to communicate as he gets older.

—*Skip Daynes*
Salt Lake City (November 2011)

Our son Tim with Yaz, his first CCI dog

Chapter 1

*W*HEN I WAS young, I remember my mother JoLee telling my brothers and sisters and me that we must listen and be perceptive in our lives. I didn't know what she meant because I only wanted to play and get milk. I looked up at a big person named Cathy and wondered why she was so big and made funny noises from her mouth. She would lift up my brothers and sisters to show them to other big people. Soon my brothers and sisters were gone and I was sad. Maybe she was saving me for something special.

Cathy kept me longer than my brothers and sisters and as I grew she took me away from my mother JoLee for little visits with other big people and talked to me from her mouth. She would ask me to "sit," "stand," "stay," "heal," and—words I really liked—"better go now." That meant I could go outside and do my business. I was only a puppy but I learned many things.

One day, Cathy put me in a small crate and lifted me up into the back of a big box with wheels (which everyone called a "car"). We bounced around and I was very scared. Where was my mother? When could I get under her soft tummy and peek out only when I wanted to. I started to cry. Where am I going? Who were these big people that talked soft and made the wheel thing bounce and make noise?

I soon fell asleep and it got dark. We stopped in a place that looked dark at first, but then it turned into light. There were big sounds like rushing wind. Cathy took me on a string, called a "leash," into a place with lots of big people. Soon we got in a line and got on a giant tube with wheels. Oh no, the tube is moving and I am in it! At first it was very hard on my ears. Where is my mommy? After a long time, the giant tube stopped moving, the door opened, and Cathy and I went out. The big people called it a "plane." It had bad smells. I rushed to the grass to do a "better go now."

I got in another car with a man in front and, after a short ride, we stopped again. I jumped out when the door opened. Cathy was happy to see the family waiting for me. There were many sounds, some high ones like when I would bite my sister when she tried to get my milk tube away. Finally the noise stopped. Two dogs, Flora and Dutchie, were there and wanted to smell my tail. One said, "Who are you?" The other said, "Are you staying here with our dad and mom?" I smelled their tails and couldn't recognize either one. Other big people held me up. One was named Susan. I liked her. There was a big one with a soft low voice. I liked him, too. Cathy lifted me up, and I thought we were going to leave again. She loved me and I loved her. She put her mouth on me and then put me down. When Cathy left, she took Florabell with her. She looked like my mom JoLee. I cried and wondered what was going to happen next.

Colonel and his siblings, fast asleep. (Colonel is second from the left.)

I soon learned that I had a place with these new people. My mother JoLee wanted me to be perceptive. Was this more of my training? I was in another, even bigger box called a "house" where I must stay for a while. This box didn't have wheels. I liked my new friend Dutchie. Dutchie didn't look much like my mother. She had tighter fur and it was white-colored. She was a little older than me. Dutchie had been a puppy like me when she came to these new people. Then she went back to California for a little while (like Florabell just did with Cathy), and then was brought back home again. Dutchie liked to get out the door and run. I watched the soft voice and Susan chase her out the door and hoped some day to see where she liked to go.

Soon I learned that the soft voice was the dad and that there were three other voices who liked me. They smelled like Susan, whom I learned was the mother. The three other voices must have been their children—like my brothers and sisters. One of the three was like Susan and held me tight. The others were more like the dad and gave me treats. I liked doing my tricks. More treats would come. Soon I felt OK about my new place. It was my new home. It was in a place called Salt Lake City, Utah.

Author's Note

Our beautiful Salt Lake City began, as noted by its founder, the great Mormon prophet Brigham Young, as "This is the Place." What a place it has become. The crossroads of the West, with beautiful mountains surrounding the valley as a protection from the "outside." Salt Lake City is noted as the ski capital of the world, hosting the most successful 2002 Winter Olympics. The sunsets over the Great Salt Lake are stunning. Business is good, with two of Utah's cities noted as the "best place to live" by several magazines. The weather is cold in the winter and hot in the summer. There is every kind of beauty in Utah, from the Desert of the Salt Flats, surrounded by alkaline and sagebrush, to Utah's Dixie in the south where people go for warmth and the beautiful Zion's Canyon. The Church of Jesus Christ of Latter-day Saints has made a wonderful impact with family values and clean, prosperous cities throughout Utah. Often, economic trends take their time to affect beautiful Utah. We are prepared for almost anything. Even our political outlook is solid. Utah has a "rainy day" fund and sometimes uses a little in an emergency. It always is replaced.

Puppies come to various cities under the direction of Canine Companions for Independence in California. Utah has several puppy raisers that are interviewed prior to receiving their puppy. Cathy Phillips is one of the great raisers of puppies. Everyone looks for Cathy's puppies. We are very lucky to have Colonel, one of Cathy's best.

A first family portrait: Skip, Colonel, Dutchie and Susan

Chapter 2

I HEARD MY NEW big dad and mom talk about CCI. That must have been where I was raised as a baby. I was on loan in this new home for a while to learn more about perception. Then I could go back to see my real mom, JoLee.

Susan called out, "Skip, take Colonel on a walk." I must be Colonel. Skip must be dad. I was from the "C" litter and remember Cathy calling me that name. I liked being Colonel—it was cool and sounded important.

I did the same things that I like each day, over and over. My food came early in the morning, "better go now" was right after, then I slept on a nice soft thing that was called a "bed." Sometimes when Mom and Dad were gone I slept in my little box, called a crate." I liked my crate; it felt safe. Dad comes home when it was still light. It was fun to see him. I'd jump and jump and he'd give me an orange thing with tails. Mom and Dad called them "carrots." I played with Dutchie during most of the light time.

Dad would give me my dinner and then we would often go in the smelly, bouncy box called a "car" to see many other dogs my age. We would all be in a room doing tricks. We didn't get treats very often. I always listened and thought, "I am learning my real mom's big word, 'perception.'" I thought it meant to know what the big people were thinking. If I knew, then my tricks were easier and Mom and Dad would smile at me and put their paws on me. It felt good. Learning new things was fun. Some of my new friends didn't listen very well and didn't get treats. A loud voice told us what to do and we walked around in the room making the big people happy. Susan and Skip took me to see my new friends many times in the car with wheels.

Back when I was with Cathy at CCI, I heard about a famous dog named Yazanoff II. I think he went on the same trip as a "graduate" dog with Tim, Susan and Skip's son. I met Tim, but he had another dog named Ehreth.

Ehreth told me Yaz went to the Rainbow Bridge. I didn't know where that was.

I could jump up in the back of the car and soon loved to go places. Mom and Dad had a thin box on the wall that shot out moving pictures and made many sounds. They seemed happy to look at the box to see and hear things. I think I saw me in there. How could I get in that little box? They called it "television." I loved each day with Dutchie. She taught me lots of things about the big people. At night, my place to sleep was on the big bed by Dad. When he rubbed my ears, I fell asleep.

One day, some cold white stuff was outside. It was very cold on my paws and tasted like cold water. I could jump high and land without hurting my tummy. The white stuff was called "snow." Some days it was too cold to go in the snow.

Author's Note

Colonel loved to have his paws rubbed. Dogs don't have thumbs; therefore all must be done with the paws. They hold a bone with them. Each finger does its job, and Colonel liked to hold up his front legs for paw rubs. A good paw-rubber person would get his attention and Colonel would never forget.

Christmas is a special time in Salt Lake City. Temple Square is filled with lights and Nativity scenes. Thousands of visitors and residents make the annual trek to the city for the Christmas program in the Conference Center. This building will hold 21,000 and is packed each night. Almost all homes are decked with lights and the feeling of peace and good will abounds.

A special day came when Mom and Dad put a tree in our house. It had lights on it that blinked. I had to close my eyes sometimes. It was like the thin box on the wall that talked and made noises. Everyone looked at that light but didn't close their eyes. My favorite time was when Dad would give me a new toy. I got lots of toys under that tree one morning. I called them babies because they were small and furry and like my brothers and sisters when they came out of Mom JoLee. I loved to hold them and carry them around. Dutchie would take them from me and rip them up. It made me sad, but Dad would fix them. I liked to go upstairs to the bed. I would stand on the bottom stair of the staircase,holding my little black dog toy, hoping the big people would see me and come upstairs with me to the big bed.

My life was full of exciting things, but my favorite was food time. Dutchie and I had dishes that were shiny. We had to sit before Dad or Mom would feed us. After food, we often went on a walk. It was hard to take walks in the white stuff. It got in my paws. We all know the word "walk" because when we go, we can read our mail on each tree around our neighborhood. When dogs take walks, they pee on trees. Each one leaves a different scent, and they all mean something to other dogs. I would respond to these messages by peeing on the same tree. This is what we call reading our mail.

Author's Note

Dogs perk up their ears about one-half inch and make a very special look on their faces when they hear a special word that they love.

Soon the things came up from the ground and it felt warm again. I got in the dirt and Mom gave me a bath in water. I like water, but not as much as Dutchie does. She just puts her paws in it and makes the water go everywhere. Dutchie is very active and always has a game to play. She is my new best friend.

I am grown up now and am smart in my classes. I get lots of treats and have lots of toy animals. Sometimes I can hold two in my mouth. My puppy teacher uses me as an example for others. I love doing things for people.

Chapter 3

Author's Note

A puppy raiser's job is to take their loaned puppy to classes, pay for shots and keep each puppy clean and happy. The Daynes family has been committed to this program for special reasons that you will note from Colonel's language later in his story. We love to teach puppies the basics, but always worry that we are missing something in their training that will be noticed after we return a puppy for advanced training. It is bittersweet for each host puppy family. We love each so much and then must take them back to CCI in Southern California where they stay often for another six months. If they graduate, they are matched with a handicapped recipient—people of many ages and backgrounds. Their life becomes very different than any normal dog because they are "life savers" to their new master and often claimed as the reason to continue to live in a most difficult world.

*T*IME GOES BY, and Mom and Dad pack up my toys and put me in the crate and in the car. I wonder where we are going because Dutchie is still home. It is a long trip and we finally arrive. The area looks very familiar to me and soon the smells also are familiar. It must be CCI. Maybe I can see my mother JoLee. Some other dogs are arriving in cars. It could be a wonderful party. Mom looks sad and Dad has tears in his eyes. It must not be a party. All of the people are in the same room with their dogs and people with loud voices arrive with no dogs. They take us each, one at a time, to kennels. I looked back at Mom and Dad with tears in their eyes. Will I ever see them again?

Before I went into the kennel, I heard that Mom and Dad found a little puppy to take back on their long ride home. Her name was Alba.

I am looking for my Mom JoLee but don't find her. My kennel mate is also sad. We are back for team training. Now we must learn to be service dogs and do our best to graduate. If we graduate we are assigned a new master. The new master depends on us to be their helper for almost everything. We need to pull wheelchairs, pick up things, open and close doors, turn on and off lights, go shopping in stores for food, and know how to do the command "visit." If we graduate, we go everywhere and go under the table at restaurants, fly on planes under our master's seat, and wear a blue CCI pack and cape. This pack is known throughout the world and we are recognized as special dogs. It is a wonderful honor to graduate. Most of us will not learn all the commands to perfection. Many will not graduate.

Each day was a special routine. We have an assigned trainer. My trainer's name was Todd. He started each morning checking me to see that I was clean and my groom was good. I had my breakfast with my kennel mate Sammy. Sammy was a Golden Retriever like me. I learned that I had been fixed as a puppy in order to calm me down and keep me focused on learning. Todd checked my basic training from Mom and Dad ("heel," "sit," "stand," "stay," "here," "down," and other basic commands). He started teaching me to jump up on a table, go under a table and stay, turn on and off lights, and many other individual commands. When we were with other dogs, we learned to lie down all at once, called "settle." We had playtime each day and then had our dinner. Sammy and I would then go to our kennel to sleep. We had "better go now" on leash before bed. It was hard to go in circles and do our business in front of people.

All of these things must be to prepare us to graduate. Some of our friends left to go back to their puppy-raising moms and dads after a few sleeps. (That is a few days in dog talk.) Sammy and I kept our schedule, and it seemed that Sammy was slow at learning some things and I feared that he would soon go away. I tried to help him learn the "down light" was on and "up light" was off. We learned about "lap," jumping up carefully with our paws across the lap of our trainer. "Visit" was my favorite. That was when I just put my head on the lap of Todd until he said "off." Many times we went to busy places where there were people. It was important to not poop unless we were told, and only when on our leashes.

The weeks went by and Sammy went back to his puppy-raising dad and mom after ten weeks. I got a new littermate. His name was Josh. Josh was not like Sammy. He was a mixture of a Golden Retriever and Yellow Lab. I liked him. He was very happy all the time and wanted to play. Josh could jump very high and loved to play during playtime. He had a big body with long legs. I think Josh was very smart and took to the training fast. Todd was impressed with Josh. I always liked to greet Todd and smile. Sometimes I would jump up and hope he would hold me while standing on my two back legs. I was good at hopping on two legs. Todd always said "down" and "don't." I felt bad and thought he didn't love me as much as Josh. My training in pulling wheelchairs was hard. I had the strength in my legs but always thought the wheel would crush my paws. I needed to pull out and forward at the same time.

The director of the Southwest region had red hair, even redder than mine. She was very nice and loved all of us. We knew it was getting close to our final testing. Many of my friends had already gone back to their puppy-raising dads and moms and some had been sent other places. Josh was very excited to take the final test, as was I. It seemed that Todd was less interested in me than Josh. He finally took me by myself and told me that he had tried to stop my anxious greeting but I just couldn't change. This was not bad for a Golden like me because I only wanted to show my love to those that loved me. But it was bad for a graduate dog helping someone in a wheelchair. I felt very low. What would happen to me now? Would they send me out to some unfamiliar place or could I go back to Mom and Dad? Would Josh graduate? Would I ever see Todd again? I still wanted to see my mom JoLee.

Chapter 4

I T WAS A secret from Dad that I was coming home. Mom
got the call from CCI saying that one of the Utah puppy raisers was just leaving with a dog from Oceanside
and could bring Colonel to Salt Lake. I only knew that Todd
told me that I was going home again. I hoped it would be with
Dutchie and Florabell. A lady and a man put me in the back of
her car and we started the trip early in the morning. I got out
once for "better go now," which had been changed to the "hur-
ry" command in team training. We stopped to walk around
and I had my food.

The car bounced along until we stopped again while the
two people got out and went into a building. They soon came
back and we were off again. It was almost night when the car
stopped. I recognized the driveway. I WAS HOME AGAIN.
The door opened and Susan, Dutchie, and Florabell were there
to greet me. There was also the light-colored Golden named
Alba. I was very happy, but where was Dad? Maybe this was the
secret. Florabell would hide and Dad would come home from

work and then I could greet him. I remembered what Todd said about my anxious greeting, but for Dad, I loved him so, I would do my normal greet.

It was getting dark and I knew Florabell would hide for Dad's big surprise. Sure enough, his car came in the driveway and I could hardly wait. The door opened and I jumped up and down. He kept saying "Flora, don't jump, don't jump." Then it dawned on him....I was Colonel! Oh, how pleased he was. We loved each other and cried. I was truly back.

Author's Note

Dogs' tails communicate their emotions. They wag fast when they are happy and get treats and food. When they are interested in something outside or hear a noise, the tail goes up. When sad, the tail goes between their legs. If it droops, sometimes they have pain, but they will never complain. Colonel wagged his tail slowly when he walked in the hospitals. It showed his love for his work.

I was happy to see my toys and sleep on the bed by Dad. I knew I had learned many things and hoped I could show them to Florabell and Dutchie. I was sure Dutchie wouldn't care, but Florabell would be interested. She liked to lick everyone. I tried to tell her people might not like all those licks. She couldn't stop, just like I couldn't stop jumping up to see my favorite people. Alba just smiled and wagged her tail.

I finally got back to normal and got my food, which is my favorite thing. Most of the time, Dad feeds me early in the morning. Sometimes, I can speak and fool him into feeding me early in the afternoon instead of later. Mom is her same old self, calling about things for me to do. Both Mom and Dad were very impressed with Todd's progress letter and how grown up I had become in six months.

Tim's beloved Yazanoff II, the first CCI service dog in Utah.

Chapter 5

Author's Note

Intermountain Therapy Animals (ITA) is an organization much like Canine Companions for Independence (CCI), and the Utah headquarters office is operated by executive director, Kathy Klotz. ITA sends "pet partner" teams to do therapy in hospitals and many other places, and has more than 300 teams in Utah, Idaho, Montana, and Nevada. Susan is a member of ITA and also runs a tennis pro shop and sells tennis things. She wanted to give Colonel a chance to be a therapy dog because he was very smart. Dutchie, Florabell, and Alba did not have the learning abilities like Colonel.

_M_OM SUSAN DECIDED to take me to ITA. It was a special place for dogs. First I needed to pass their test. I needed to sit, stay, heel and not be distracted by other dogs near me. I must have a good disposition and show good skills of perception. My Mom JoLee taught me perception when I was a puppy. I remembered perception with Todd and always had a great interest in trying to understand what humans needed. I loved going to ITA and taking the test. I passed it easily. I got a red cape with my name on it, and Mom got a special identification badge to recognize that I was a licensed "therapy" dog.

I started in the University Medical Center Rehab. Mom and I thought that Rehab would be good for us because her youngest son, Tim had been in Rehab for six months. Tim was injured at Lake Powell when he was 16 years old and is a quadriplegic. Tim got the first CCI service dog in Utah. His name was Yazanoff II. I heard stories about Yaz during team training. He was the all-time best service dog to graduate.

A nurse introduced me to the first patient. Jimmy was a young boy who had trouble holding things. His muscles were weak and he looked very pale. First, I sat in a chair by him so that he could see that I came to help. I love to sit on chairs. The rehab lady wanted him to develop coordination in his arms and hands. We then sat on a blanket and Mom took out some grooming tools and he started to brush my coat. It felt good but his hands were slow. He dropped the brush and I picked it up for him and put it in his lap. He smiled. After a while, I felt like he wanted to pat me instead of brush. I snuggled closer to him and he started to pat me with both arms. He held me tight and put his head close to mine. I think that the rehab lady was happy. Jimmy smiled and we left after I did my food on nose trick. He liked that trick. We left and I decided that I liked being a therapy dog.

The next visit was in another room. A little girl was in a bed and she had lots of tubes hanging around her. Her name was Ellina. She couldn't talk but I knew she loved dogs because she smiled at me. I sat on a chair near her bed and wagged my tail. It hit the chair and made a tapping noise. Soon the nurse agreed to let me get into bed with Ellina. I was very careful and crawled through the tubes and wires so as not to disturb them. I lay my head on her chest and looked up into her eyes. She was saying, with her eyes, that she loved me. I knew she did. I wanted to stay longer, but the nurse told Mom that I must get down. I told Ellina that I would be back. She understood.

We chose to keep visiting the University Hospital and saw Jimmy and Ellina various times. Jimmy got stronger and we started to play ball and tug. It was fun. He was talking and laughing and after a few weeks he went home. Before going home, he made me a card and said he loved me and hoped to see me again.

Ellina was different. She had a disease of her lungs and had a hard time breathing. Dogs breathe with their diaphragm. We always take big breaths and sometimes make loud heaving noises when we are running or excited and playing. I tried to understand what Ellina needed. It seems she needed more air and her mouth could not get it in. They had a tube in her nose. I am sure it was very uncomfortable. Dogs' noses can smell many times better than humans and they are bigger. We would never need tubes.

Finally Ellina was out of the bed and in a wheelchair. It had wheels like the car, but thinner. A big person had to push the chair. Ellina still had some tubes in her. She could talk sometimes when some of the tubes were out. I loved her and wanted her to play. She met us once a week in Rehab. Each week she looked stronger and finally we played tug. I almost pulled her out of her chair.

They took her out and sat her on a bed on the floor. Then I got closer to her and did my "visit" command. This is when I put my head in her lap and looked up at her. Her eyes were very bright now and she talked funny. It was not like Dad and Mom. We came the next week and she was gone.

One day I saw a lady who looked very sad. I don't remember her name, but I knew she needed me. There were lots of wires and tubes coming from her but her eyes told me to come closer. I got on the chair and carefully got into her bed. She could talk and said that she wanted to feel my face next to hers. I know she had a dog at her home because she was not afraid. Mom put a cookie in her mouth and I carefully took it out while she held it still for me. Mom said, "take it nicely." That is one of the commands that Todd taught me. I did it two times. The cookies were good but the tears in her eyes were even better. I knew she loved me and I wanted to come back again.

I had lots of visits during the hot time, then it started to be cold. I was so glad to see Dad come home each day at almost dark. Sometimes the four of us—Florabell, Dutchie, Alba and me—would go for a walk around the neighborhood. We read our mail and peed on trees. We took shorter walks because it was cold.

Each of us was very different. Dutchie would try to get away from Mom and Dad when the door opened. Florabell liked to talk to me and make me happy. She was very sweet and was like my mother JoLee. Alba was just learning the basic things and was still going to puppy classes. She was getting bigger. Her fur was very fine and the white blaze on her chest was pretty. She looked at me a lot with her big, beautiful eyes. As it got colder, I got colder. My coat started to grow thicker and I felt better.

I really liked my toys. I called them "babies" because that's what Dad called them. I had 20 babies. My favorite was a little black dog. He always would bark until Dutchie chewed out the inside. Dad always fixed my babies. He has a pointed little sharp thing in his office and strings hooks on it. The sharp thing goes in and out of my babies and soon they can play again.

Author's Note

Colonel watched every move I made. Sometimes he watched me at night while I slept. Dogs stare at their masters. They are looking for signs that all is OK. This is another method of showing unconditional love. Dogs read our mood from a thousand tell-tales that we do not recognize in ourselves. They read us with something like a psychic perception.

Here I am visiting with my dad's sister, Karen Daynes, who was in the Huntsman Cancer Institute being treated for ovarian cancer. Taking pictures of patients at Huntsman is not permitted, so you can only see her hand. This picture was taken by Lisa Markin, a friend visiting from Canada to observe me making my rounds.

Chapter 6

I WAS THREE YEARS old when Mom and I decided to go do therapy more than once a week. Some of the nurses at the University Medical Center would call my name and I would jump up with my feet on the counter and smile while my tail was moving really fast. One day Mom was called to see a little girl. Her name was Ashley. Mom heard that Ashley and her mother were hit by a car and burned. They lived in a far-away city. Now Ashley was in a bed where I went lots of times. It seems Ashley had been under the car and burned by a hot pipe on her face.

When I first saw Ashley, her face looked like the black Lab in CCI who got mud on her face and it wouldn't wash off easily. Ashley had a funny smell, but I knew I would love her right away. The nurse said I could get in bed with her. Oh boy. I love to go into beds. I put my head on her chest and could see that she was surprised. Why was she not smiling? Maybe her mouth was sore from eating a big bone. She looked in my eyes and I could see tears in hers. Why was she sad? I always make children feel happy.

The second visit was just like the first. Ashley still had tears but she held me tight. Her hands were very expressive. They moved around my face and neck with softness and much love. Mom decided to visit each day. Ashley wouldn't get out of bed. It was hard for her to move. I put my paw on her to let her know I wanted to take some of her pain. I loved Ashley and knew soon her eyes would smile.

After a few sleeps and visits, her eyes smiled but darted back and forth. It was like when mom JoLee was looking for Annie, her funny little puppy that couldn't ever find the milk tube. Sometimes it took a long time to find Annie with her eyes, because she couldn't move with all of the rest of us hooked on her milk tubes.

Colonel with Ashley in the University of Utah Hospital Burn ICU.

Something was wrong with Ashley. They were always doing something to her legs or putting patches on her face. It made the tears come. Ashley just stayed in the bed. She cried sometimes and her Dad wanted her to be able to get down from the bed like I do. I wanted to stay at night with her to keep her from crying, but I needed my apple that I share with Florabell, Dutchie and Alba before going to my bed at home.

One day, a week later, Ashley came out of her bed and took me for a little walk in the room. Everyone was excited and some

clapped their hands. Ashley's mother was very happy. She had some smelly cloth things on her arms. I heard that the same car also hit her. The nurse wanted more walk time and I wanted it too. Ashley started to do more walks and we went around the floor and passed other rooms. Ashley had a birthday party and I was invited and wore a birthday hat. I jumped up on her bed and we had great fun. I got cake and Mom let me eat it. Ashley was nine years old.

I want to always go with Ashley on walks. Her hands were very soft with my leash. I know she loved me and wanted me to be with her every day. Mom said that soon she would be able to go in the car back to Boise. I don't know what Boise is but think it is like a big city with many lights and cars and noise.

I knew Ashley did not like to look at her face in the mirror. I loved her anyway. It seemed

that Ashley needed to get out of bed because the doctors were talking about her legs not moving for a long time. Many skin grafts on her face had been taken from her legs. The doctors were concerned that infection would cause major problems if she did not walk. I was sad because Ashley went home. She would come back to see me because we were good friends.

Two times a week, on Wednesdays and Fridays, I go to the University Hospital, and soon Mom says I can go to a hospital nearby for children. I like children.

Chapter 7

*M*Y FRIEND DIANE came this morning, like she does every Wednesday and Friday, to go with Mom on a run. Mom and Diane have been running for many years. They always take us. Dutchie tries to run in the middle of the road with Mom and I run with Diane. Sometimes Alba stays home.

Diane is a very cool lady. She is married to Dave and he has a big ranch with horses and some cows. Dad says their ranch is located in a beautiful part of the upper Provo River drainage and has good smells during the summer. It is called the Hewlett Ranch. There are some cabins up there, but Dave and Diane's place is like a beautiful western house. They also have a cabin and lots of land for the Epperson children. Mom and Diane talk most of the time while we run. I can understand some of the things, especially when they talk about food. It was still winter, but warmer. Some days the air started blowing cold, then it would stop. The heat would come some day. I remember that as it got warmer, I turned three.

Ehreth, Tim's service dog, liked dog pizzas and liked parties. He came over to our house and we had a wonderful birthday party for me. My birthday is March 28th. I wore the hat that Ashley gave me, and I ate the first bite of dog pizza. Ehreth is getting a bump on top of his head. Tim and Karen don't know what it is, but I do. Later in my story I will tell more about Ehreth. We had five at my party not counting Karen, Tim, Mom and Dad. I like Karen and Tim.

Tim had a smell like Dad and Mom. He was in one of those chairs with wheels. I liked to "jump up on" his lap. I put my paws across his lap and stretched my body until my back paws almost lifted off the ground. We went on long walks with Ehreth. He was very much liked by important big people. When Tim got his Master's Degree from the University of Utah, Ehreth was there in all the pictures.

I love my family and friends but I miss Todd. I hope he is proud that I am learning the word my mother JoLee told me about. Perception must be doing what the big people need when they don't give any commands. It comes to me easily in my work.

I want to help hospital people that call to me. Mom and the nurses often don't hear their call and soon I am walking to another area.

Author's Note

===================================

Dogs do not deceive, do not betray, and do not covet.

===================================

One time a big person with many tubes called me in my intuition. He needed me very much so I stopped in front of his door and dug my nails into the floor. Mom tried to pull me, but I stayed strong. She did not know this person but took me in the room. His eyes said please come on my bed. I found a chair and jumped up but it was far away from the bed. Mom pulled it closer and I carefully climbed in. I went under some tubes and over some. Finally I came close to his face. Tears were in his eyes, his hands couldn't move. His neck had a tube in it and I was a little afraid but I stayed very still.

A nurse came in and saw Mom and me. She was very pleased and saw the tears. Later she told Mom that the man had his dog in the car and a terrible crash came. He did not know where his dog was. Could I find him? Where would he be? Mom said that he was OK and staying in a special hospital for dogs. Then I knew why it was important for me to see this nice man.

There was a special lady in charge of our teams. We were called ITA (Intermountain Therapy Animals). ITA had some cats and a bird and bunny. We had a meeting later when it was warm in a park. The lady's name was Kathy, just like my first friend at CCI. She spoke to many dogs and we all understood her words. She smelled very good and had lots of treats and toys. Sometimes she had ice cubes for all of her dog friends, too. I met many dogs at the party but I couldn't wear my hat. Kathy gave me a thing to hang on my collar. It said "Dog of the Year 2003." I like this new Kathy because she loves all animals and is very smart. Now I am an ITA dog and Kathy is proud of me. I wear a red cape with my name on it and love to go anywhere Kathy sends me.

There is a special house that dogs like, where Kathy spends her time during the day. Other ladies live there in the day and help us with our parties and keep new dogs coming for accreditation. I like to go for visits to Kathy's day house. She has a cat that races around and is not afraid of me. Kathy has trained the best dogs in Utah. She is just like my favorite Cathy in California.

Mom said I could go to another hospital before the children place. It was OK with Kathy. It had a funny name, "LDS Hospital." I would work in the Rehab. There were many visits at LDS, and one time I helped an older man who was sleeping all the time. I would get from my chair on his bed and crawl up to his chest. Each time I put my head near his I could hear him thinking. I know he wanted to wake up and talk to me. After a few visits he did wake up and said "my dog." He loved his dog and missed him. Later he told my Mom that I should be a "five-star General instead of a Colonel.

LDS had a party at a big house each year and I always went. I liked the smell of the food. Ladies brought it to our tables. Mom wouldn't let me sit on a chair with the food in front of me. Maybe Dad will let me, if he comes to the parties. I always get to go up in front of the people and speak. It is fun and they make noises with their hands after I speak.

This is one of my favorite pictures—me sitting in Dad's chair at the store.

My Dad has a big store. Sometimes he takes me out and brings me back without any visits. There are no nurses at his store. He has funny big instruments that make chiming sounds when you push on the white and black things. There are lots of those chiming things. Dad's office has a picture of me playing one of the pianos. It also has a picture of all of his family and dogs. I sit in Dad's big chair and wait for him to call me. It makes me feel very important to sit on Dad's chair. I think I can put my paws on those white and black things and make chimes. Dad says he can teach me to play the piano.

I am not sure why Dutchie, Alba, and Florabell were not doing visits like me. They stayed home most of the time but always asked about my new friends at the hospitals.

I want to tell the story about Florabell. She came home from CCI before I did. I was still in training but never much saw her because she went to the training center in Northern California. Dad went to pick up Florabell in southern California. She was released because she was neurotic. I wish I had seen her. It wasn't her fault. The director had taken her to the Northern California center as a show dog. Florabell was very pretty and obedient. She was perfect until they shipped her back to the Southern California center. Someone left her alone in her kennel. Florabell was lonely and jumped up to see other dogs catching her teeth on a top wire and breaking off one. It was very painful and she became agitated.

Dad needed to deliver a piano in Colorado City, Utah. He had a trailer behind his big car and left the trailer in St. George, then drove on to pick up Florabell. She was so glad to see him that she squealed and ran around in circles for a long time. Of course she licked and licked. They wouldn't let Dad see me while I was in training. After driving to St. George, Utah, Dad hooked up the trailer and went to Colorado City to drop off the white baby grand.

It was very hot and he took Florabell out of the car and asked for a bowl of water for her. She thought that he was leaving her with the strange ladies that sat on a couch and nursed babies. Dad delivered the grand piano by himself and hurried to finish because he knew what Florabell was thinking. She was very happy to get back into the big cool car and pull away from Colorado City.

I was so pleased to see Florabell after Dad's big surprise. Now we had four of us again. Florabell had learned many things and helped me learn even more on my visits. I loved Florabell very much.

I was now 5 years old. In dog years that was 35. I felt important and I remember Mom has arranged to also go to Primary Children's Hospital. I also went to the Residential Treatment Center, a branch of the Primary hospital in Research Park. Mom took me to dog shows and I participated, but when Dad was there I would bring him the toy instead of follow the rules to get points from the judge. I could smell Dad even though he was hiding far away.

Author's Note

Dogs have very sensitive noses and can smell the scent of a friend often two hundred yards away.

Primary Children's Hospital smells different than the others and there are bright colors and little voices. The children that come here are very sick and come from many miles in cars that bounce. Some even come on the noisy planes. Nurse Barnes is in charge of Rehab.

She loves me and knows about my perception. Mom talks nice to her like friends do. She always has a child with problems for me to see. Most of the time they are in a chair with wheels then they get out and go down with me. I know that I must be very careful when the little ones are near me. I am often bigger than them and at first they look scared in their eyes.

My years working at University, Primary, LDS, and Residential were always very busy.

17A Calendar Dogs

Colonel & Flora — September 2002

2004 — Colonel and Alba

March 2003

2005 — Colonel and Alba February

Colonel 2006 — February

Chapter 8

*N*OW I MUST tell more about the Daynes family, consisting of a daughter and two sons. My favorite was Tim. I understood him best because he had a CCI service dog named Ehreth. Every time I saw Tim he was in a wheelchair. I learned about wheelchairs at Primary. People that can't move their legs live in those chairs. How do they get in their beds? Tim has a nice lady with dark hair that comes with him. She knows everything about dogs. Her name is Karen and she loves Ehreth.

Tim is very smart and has papers that show he is special. Karen has a nice home with other dogs that live there. A new one is Gia. Gia is a chocolate Lab and can't think very well. She likes her food and any other food she can find. Gia barks a lot and people just don't know what she is saying. I know she was injured when she was a puppy and didn't get enough air in her lungs. She says over and over "help me, help me." She wants more food. She is very good at looking for it and very strong.

Tim and Karen's home has good smells from dogs and a couch that has a cover on it. Gia ate the insides of the couch and her tummy hurt for a long time.

Tracy, the girl in our family, had good smells. She was a lot like Mom. She held me close and kissed me. Then she was gone. She went out of our house many times with other people. I think everyone loves Tracy. She moved away with her mate. His name was John. They live far away and have a family. Britni is the oldest girl, then Shelbi, and there is a boy named Hunter.

Todd was the oldest boy. His name was the same as my trainer but he didn't know much about dogs. I loved Todd and hoped he loved me, too. He was very smart and his brain was always working. He knew all about perception. Todd, the oldest brother, was going to big-people school and liked it. Todd found a mate named Andrea. They had babies and live fairly close to our house. The oldest is Brandon, then John, then Abby, and the youngest is David.

Daynes family dogs go hiking in the mountains.
(From left:) Gia, Colonel, Alba, Flora, Dutchie, Ehreth and Max

Todd's daughter Abigail loves dogs. Her love of dogs started when she was a baby. One day Dad was tending her and she was only two years old. Dutchie was helping while Dad was putting a kid's video on the light that comes from the wall. Abigail decided to lay on Dutchie and also thought she would like to take a bite out of her. Dutchie made a loud squeal and jumped with Abigail on her. Abigail cried for just a few minutes, then started playing again with Dutchie. That is when I knew she was a dog girl. She just started her education of how dogs think and soon will be learning about perception.

Abby is now older and says she wants to have a home with many dogs when she can. She now only has Mo, a Puggle. Mo is small and loves to play. He once had a collar that make him stay in a certain area. His mom Andrea put him in her car and drove out of the house area while he cried.

Tim went to school in a bus and he finally stayed up by the mountains in a big tall building. He was on the bottom floor and near the room where Susan's friend Coach stayed. While he was in the tall building he met Karen and they became friends. Now she loves Tim and feeds him his food. They live close to Dad's house and we often go on walks with Tim and Karen's three dogs. It looks like a whole pack of dogs going around the neighborhood.

A man named Ben came to our house. He was very nice and had a funny box in his hand (they called it a "camera") that pointed to me most of the time. He followed Mom and I around with his box to Primary, LDS and the University Hospital. I found out that the little box could remember everything and put it up on the light thing on our wall. I saw myself up there and Mom and nurses and everything. It was a wonderful box. Sometimes Mom would show the pictures in the box to others. They liked to see my tail wagging and how I worked. I have asked Dad to put lots of pictures in the middle of my story. You can look at them and see some of my friends.

The Psychiatric Ward was my most interesting visit. There was a big room and chairs around the room and people sitting in some of the chairs. There was a chair between the people. Some looked at me very funny and some looked up at the ceiling and some looked at the floor. I couldn't get any to focus on me at first.

Mom and I decided that I should get in the chair next to a person. When I jumped up the nearest person laughed and pointed at me. Mom thought I should get a treat so she gave the happy person a cookie for me. I liked it. I went to every vacant chair and soon the whole group was pointing and laughing. It was good to see them focus on something together. The nurse was very happy with my visit and wanted me to come back again.

I think I am doing more good things here than anywhere I go. I have made friends with all of the patients. In fact, one very sweet lady asked me to come up on her lap. Mom gave me the command "On my lap," and I went up very carefully. She held me close and asked to have a picture taken. I love pictures and always get good ones because of my experience with Ben and his box. After the picture she said that when she went home if she was sad she could look at the picture and feel happy again.

It seems that the patients in Psychiatric all asked the nurses to have me come back soon so they made a picture of me. The words under the picture said, "Colonel is coming today." It had a big smile on my face. The other picture was "Colonel is on vacation." It was up when I was at another hospital. I loved going to see my friends at Psychiatric better than anywhere and wanted to be with them every day.

Chapter 9

A TERRIBLE THING HAPPENED when I was seven years old. Mom and Dad had gone to Hawaii, like they do every year, and Rocio was tending us. Rocio lived in our home and often took us to grooming and walks. We all loved Rocio; she was from Peru but talked to us mostly in English.

Florabell started to cough and couldn't stop. Some liquid came out of her mouth and Rocio called Dad and Mom. Dad said he would come home fast. The next day Florabell was worse. The liquid turned red and she was very weak. Dutchie, Alba and I tried to help her but we couldn't do anything but lie down by her and tell her Dad would be home soon. Finally, that evening she stopped breathing and was cold. Dad arrived in the morning and was very sad. We were all sad because Dad and Mom were not home to hold her and love her.

Dad took her to the University Vet and we got a little box back, with her in it. I don't know when you stop breathing how you can fit in that little box. We planted a beautiful tree in the front yard with a nice plaque that stuck in the ground that had "Florabell" written on it.

Author's Note

Dogs mourn not just the immediate loss but also the enduring memory of what was lost. They are uncomplaining about their own suffering.

It was the hot time of the year and Dad had taken Dutchie to his boat up a big canyon to Strawberry Reservoir. She told us that it was fun and Alba wanted to go. I was older and knew Dad would invite me. Dutchie ran around and while Dad's big boat was going fast though waves and she flew in the air. She was not afraid because she is a Lab. Labs love the water.

It was finally my turn. Kerwin, Dad's vice president at his piano store, was with us. He is a very nice man and knows all about boats. We decided not to go too fast because it was my first time. I stayed close to Dad when the motors started to get us on top of the water. Soon we stopped and Dad and Kerwin started putting out funny shiny things in the water. Maybe they were telling the water to play with them and catch their toys. The boat moved slowly and Dad looked in a small box with colors every once in a while. There were strings in the water maybe they were pulling one of my toys.

I decided to get in and see. No one was looking when I stood up on my back legs, peeked at the water and jumped in. It was cold and I couldn't see any toys, just that whirling thing in the back. Soon Dad jumped into action. The motor stopped, the strings were pulled in, and Kerwin took the wheel while Dad stood on the back of the boat and called me to him. All

Goldens know how to swim, but the boat was drifting away and I needed to paddle hard. Dad reached down and got my collar and pulled me into the boat. His eyes were afraid. He was very glad I was in the boat and dried me off while he talked to me about not doing this trick again. What if Mom found out? Dad would be in BIG trouble.

We came back to our home and I told Dutchie that the water was cold. She said the next time she went she would try some water tricks. I wish Florabell were still here to tell her. She would lick me and tell me that I was very brave.

Chapter 10

I WAS EIGHT YEARS old and visiting more often at Primary Children's Hospital. Mom had a call from nurse Barnes that a little girl had been in a drowning accident and had been in the hospital a few weeks. She was still not talking or focusing on anything. Maybe I can help her. Her name was Hannah.

Mom and I first saw Hannah and she was out of her bed in a chair. She had several wires and tubes. Hannah looked very different from the other children because her eyes would not focus and they looked like milk spilled in them. The nurses and doctors were not far and all were concerned that Hannah was not progressing.

I sat in a chair near her and tried to lay my head on her lap. Most of the time I get some movement or at least a look, but nothing happened. I got off my chair and went in front of Hannah. Her mind said that she knew I was there but was held back and couldn't let her move to see me.

I got on the chair again and made a very loud burp. Hannah started to giggle, and all the people came to her side. She laughed and laughed. Mom was amazed at my burp. I know how, but am polite most of the time. Well, Hannah liked me and wanted me to come back. I wanted to let her eyes get better and climb into bed with her.

The next time we came, the nurse had a little box with a voice on it and buttons. Hannah could push the button and the box would say, "speak" then I would do a dog speak. She would laugh. This was very fun. Many of my commands were on the box and we used it many times during our visits.

One visit, the nurse stopped Mom and me at the door and said "we have a surprise." I love a surprise and hoped it would be a hat and cake to eat. We waited just a few minutes then heard "Colonel, come in." It was Hannah's real voice. Mom and

I were very happy and I wagged my tail faster than ever.

Hannah got much better and her parents were very happy. They called a person from *Parents* mag-azine and made an appointment for a party at the park. The party was for all of Hannah's friends that helped her. I was an honored guest dog. Many pictures were taken and later and article was written about the "Burping Golden Retriever that saved Hannah's life." It was in the September 2008 issue.

After Hannah went back to her home, we heard she was back in school. I was glad because school is important. I re-member learning a lot from my puppy school and my team training with Todd.

The wind was blowing again and it looked like the white stuff would come. Dutchie was ten years old and still running away any time she could get out the door. I was worried about her because she coughed a little sometimes. One day she was real bad and Mom and Dad took her to the University Dog Hospital. She didn't come back. I knew something very bad happened because Mom and Dad were very sad. Everyone loved Dutchie. Mom got a big plastic yellow Lab and put it in our family room and put Dutchie's collar on it. I smell it every once in awhile. I really miss her. Mom also had a box with Dutchie in it to put with Florabell's box.

Dad told me about the "Rainbow Bridge." It is where dogs go after they leave this earth and wait for their masters. Mom and Dad will someday look for me at the "rainbow bridge." One of Tim's dogs, Max, a beautiful, strong black Lab, went to the rainbow bridge. He always walked with us and protected us when we all got together for long walks. Ehreth also went to the rainbow bridge. I miss Ehreth very much.

• •

August 2006

We Love Colonel!

Our eight-year-old daughter, Hannah, was in a near-drowning accident on July 3, 2006. We have spent over six weeks in hospitals so far with Hannah. She is currently at Primary Children's Medical Center (PCMC) for rehabilitation services. I knew the day that I saw Colonel (the dog) and Susan (the owner) walking down the hall that we had to have Colonel visit Hannah. Hannah loves animals and I knew she would enjoy Colonel. I had no idea just how great her response would be. The first visit was special for us but Hannah wasn't able to respond. She appeared to enjoy the visit but because of the severity of her injury she had no way to convey her happiness.

On Colonel's second visit he made our daughter laugh for the first time—by burping! Hannah not only smiled but she laughed. The Occupational Therapist, the Speech Therapist, and the Physical Therapist were all co-treating, and we were all so amazed that we kept talking about it and Hannah kept smiling and laughing. Everybody in the room had tears in their eyes! We had hoped for weeks to hear Hannah's voice again and Colonel was the one who coaxed it out of her. I have never been so happy to see a smile in my entire life.

Colonel seemed to sense what Hannah needed and needs. When Susan says, "Speak," Colonel barks quietly so Hannah does not jump. Hannah is very sensitive to sound and, having a brain injury, her whole body jumps when she is the least bit startled. Colonel keeps his paw on Hannah's knee at all times to let her know that he is nearby. Colonel tolerates several strange positions (that we put him in) so that he can be closer to Hannah. Colonel does not lick or jump up on Hannah. When Colonel comes by for a visit, Hannah's whole body seems to relax. Hannah seems to know that soon the fun will begin!

Colonel can perform several entertaining tricks that keep us all laughing! We feel that Colonel's presence has contributed a great deal to Hannah's recovery. We look so forward to Wednesdays because we know we will have a chance to see Colonel and Susan. We are grateful that Susan has trained Colonel well and that we have a chance to benefit from such a wonderful program!

Colonel's kind of therapy cannot be found anywhere else.

Kirsten Sessions
Hannah's Mom

Furry Friend

On a camping trip two summers ago, Hannah Sessions, then 7, was rafting down a tranquil section of Idaho's Boise River with her dad, Brook, her brother, Cole, 10, and her grandfather, Jon Landeen. Suddenly, their inflatable craft smacked into a tree that had fallen into the river. The current pushed their raft underneath the log, plunging the entire family into the frigid water. When Brook, Cole, and Jon surfaced downstream, Hannah was nowhere in sight. After what seemed like an eternity, she popped up near the log, still wearing her life jacket. Hannah was limp and had no pulse. Hannah's dad and grandpa quickly administered CPR, restoring her heartbeat, while witnesses called for help. Within an hour, Hannah was being airlifted to St. Luke's Children's Hospital, in Boise. There, doctors delivered the bad news: Her brain had been deprived of oxygen, causing permanent dam-

paid Hannah a visit. With some assistance from [?] Kirsten, Hannah began to stroke Colonel's soft fur. [?] on for a few minutes, until the dog burped loudly i[?] nah's ear. The comic relief caused everyone in the chuckle—including Hannah. It was the first time sinc[?] cident that she had responded to outside stimuli. "St[?] and laughed several times that day," her dad recalls.

Colonel quickly became an integral part of Hanna[?] ing process. During speech sessions, she learne[?] a voice synthesizer to give him commands, like "[?] "Speak." Soon she was able to say them all by her[?] dog's presence during her grueling physical therapy [?] made them more bearable. As she learned to wal[?] ing Colonel's leash than when he wasn't around. And[?] Hannah would work a lot harder—and longer—whi[?] ing his fur helped her relax and figure out how to co[?] involuntary muscle movements.

Hannah left the hospital seven weeks later, and her[?] able recovery has continued. She walks unaided (tho[?] balance and coordination may never be normal), a[?] returned to Rosamond Elementary School.

Hannah, now 10, no longer works with Colonel, b[?] always be grateful for everything he did for her. Sh[?] to become a veterinarian someday. "He would wag[?] madly whenever he'd see me," she recalls. "Being w[?]

Parents

226 Brilliant Baby Names

Raising A Polite Kid In A Rude World

SCHOOL

Keep Yo[?] Baby Hap[?] Anywhe[?]

THE POW[?] OF NAP[?]

10 Reaso[?] To Ca[?] The Doct[?] ASA[?]

Chapter 11

*D*AD ALWAYS LOVED to take me to do "Dr. Dog." Dr. Dog is a promotional event sponsored by the University Medical Center. We have done lots of Dr. Dog presentations at short care centers sponsored by the University Medical Center during the spring. There is a long-ride one in Tooele, and a shorter one at Olympus Cove. The really big one is near the University Medical Center.

Children bring their teddy bears and I sit on a chair. I am dressed in scrubs and have a surgical hat. I often wear glasses to look like a Doctor. Dad dresses like a Doctor and Mom like a nurse. Many children come. One time there where were over 300 children with their parents. Not all had brought bears, but the hospital had some to spare.

I hold each teddy bear in my mouth while sitting on the chair and tell Dad what is wrong with it. He writes on a paper that the bear needs to be fixed where I told him. He says, "Dr. Dog says that this bear broke its foot." That is what I told him. Mom would fix the foot with a bandage and Dad would tell the child to cuddle with it at night and give it hugs. After 200 bears my mouth was very dry and I was tired.

One time at Olympus Cove I had a chance to help Dad in a big way. We had seen lots of children and both of us were tired. Mom was at a training session with a new dog we got from CCI named Tanny. The nurse was Britni, Dad's oldest granddaughter. Dad was very tired like when we went on walks and was getting pain going up his neck. He couldn't breathe very well. I knew something was very wrong with Dad. My mind told me to make him go into the back room with a real Doctor and ask him about his pain. Often Dad and I talk. I think he understands dog thinking. He went back there. The Doctor told Dad to go up to the ER at the University Hospital right away. He took Britni and me to Mom and went up.

They told Dad that he had to have an angiogram to find out if he had blocked arteries. The next day Dad was admitted to the hospital with his main artery blocked 95%, and two others. The surgeon told Dad that it was a good thing he came in when he did because in one more day he would have a heart attack. The main artery is called the "widow-maker" because it can't be fixed if it blocks totally.

Dad was operated on and had a triple bypass. He asked to see me after a few days and I got into bed with him. Dad thanked me for saving his life and we cried together tears of happiness. I love Dad and want him to come home soon. He did come home and was getting better everyday. He is much stronger now and we can go on walks again after the warm comes.

Here I am in a University of Utah medical helicopter for another Dr. Dog assignment.

Author's Note

Dogs are well aware of their—and our—mortality. We acknowledge that they have intuition. Intuition is a higher form of knowledge than instinct. It is independent of any reasoning. Their knowledge is not derived from experience. It includes understanding of spatial relationships and an awareness of time.

We got another dog named Tanny after Florabell went to Rainbow Bridge. Tanny is a funny dog. She is very pretty, but has very long ears. Tanny is small and a mixture of a Golden and yellow Lab. She runs away from Mom and can jump clear over the couch. Mom and Dad take her to puppy classes twice a week at night. Tanny says that they are fun, and she can chase all of the other dogs until they sit down because they are tired. Sometimes Tanny runs around in circles. She has too much energy and needs a big place.

Chapter 12

*I*WAS EIGHT YEARS old now and feeling very smart. That is 56 in people age. I am sure that I have learned about perception especially when Dad needed me. He could have died and gone to Rainbow Bridge to see Florabell and Dutchie. He would have seen many dogs. Dad had dogs when he worked on a ranch. The dogs were Border Collies. These dogs are very smart and can take commands to go and bring back sheep that have strayed from the herd. Dad also had Beagles, Poodles, and a Cocker Spaniel. I am glad Dad is here with me and Mom. I love Dad and he loves me. I am his favorite dog.

The University Medical Center asked Mom, Dad, and I to be special guests at a big event. It was awards to be given to important surgeons and special people for excellence in their work. The party was at a big hotel called "the Grand America." It is a five-star hotel, which Dad says is the best in Utah.

I know that I must be careful not to get too close to the food. I love the smells. Mom gave me a good groom and brushed my teeth very good. This is the biggest party I have attended and wondered if I should dress up as Dr. Dog or wear my party hat. Mom said I must be very good, and maybe I could have my own chair.

There was a big flat area with a funny silver bone that the big people talked into. It made their voices loud. Each time a new doctor would come up to the silver bone, everyone put their hands together and made noise. It must be that they were excited. I would wag my tail because I don't have hands, just paws with no thumbs. Some people said my name and my tail wagged faster. I did get a chair and hoped I would not fall off while I got into the excitement.

. . . .

(sent on Primary Children's letterhead)

August 22, 2006

To Whom It May Concern:

I am writing in regard to Colonel, who works as a therapy dog at Primary Children's Medical Center (PCMC). I am a physical therapist at PCMC, and I work in inpatient rehabilitation. Colonel and his owner, Susan Daynes, come to volunteer on our unit every Wednesday, and they are incredibly valuable assets to our team.

I have worked with several therapy dogs in my years working at PCMC, and Colonel is by far the best! He is the best-trained, the best-behaved, and the best-managed. He has been instrumental in assisting in all disciplines of therapy, including: physical therapy, occupational therapy, and speech therapy. Susan and Colonel work well with each other, with the therapists and, most importantly, with the children. Many of the kids on our unit are in the hospital for several weeks or even months. They know when Colonel comes, and they eagerly look forward to his visits. He is a wonderful motivator and a welcome friend to our patients. We are very fortunate to work with Colonel and Susan!

I would highly recommend Colonel and Susan for any award that recognizes his gifts and the services that he provides. If you have any questions or would like more specific information, please feel free to contact me at (801) 588-375. Thank you for your time and consideration in this matter.

Sincerely,

Lisa E. Barnes, PT

• •

Finally, a man called my name and Mom and I went up on the big platform by the silver bone. They gave be a big wooden plaque and said it had my name on it and it was a "Health Hero Award." I dropped it because it was very heavy and slippery. Mom picked it up and asked me to speak. Often she wants me to speak in Spanish or French or German. This time I just spoke a good bark in English. Everybody stood up and put their hands together. It was great fun.

What is a hero? It must be what my mom JoLee taught me about perception. A person that does good things when not asked and gives love to another. It is when they are thinking in their mind and doing what it says. I love doing things, especially for children and Dad.

Ben was there with his little box and said he was going to use it for a documentary about ITA with me as a HERO. I am very excited and hope I can do well for Ben.

In Appreciation

COLONEL DAYNES

*"I think dogs are the most amazing creatures; they give
unconditional love. For me they are the role model for being alive."*
Gilda Radner

For his PAWSitively stellar teamwork, service and
advocacy for the staff, patients and
families of University Hospital. We know no other
canine with the patience, love and commitment of Colonel.

Presented by
University of Utah Hospitals & Clinics Board
October 2006

Chapter 13

*B*EN WAS EXCITED about my award and wanted to get his little box going, telling stories about some of my other experiences. He came to some of the hospitals with Mom. He needed a current story about someone who needed help.

There was a bad accident with a little boy, Caleb, who was in a coma and hovering between life and death with very little brain activity. His mother and sisters had been killed in an automobile accident in which Caleb hit his head very hard and bounced back. His brain and spine were damaged and he had several broken bones.

His father was very sad and concerned that Caleb would also die. Ben decided to get permission to bring his little box to Primary Children's hospital. Lisa Barnes, the Rehab therapist, agreed to have me work with Caleb while the box was running.

My first day with Caleb was very hard. He had a scared look in his eyes. He had seen horrible things happen to his family. He was very sad and wondered where they were. I tried to help him focus on his dad and getting a little stronger to fight the pain. This can happen when I lay my head on his chest and speak to him with my inner thoughts. My eyes often can send a message of love to someone who needs it.

Caleb was lying on the floor and Lisa was trying to get him to move his arms and legs. I cuddled close to him, lying so that my back was close to his tummy and my head was near his head. Mom puts dog perfume on me. It is not too cool but lots of sad people smile with their smaller noses. Alba thinks I stink and tries to make me roll in dirt. It only took a few minutes lying by Caleb when my perception said that if I got even closer, he would lift up his arm to hold me.

I was right; Caleb lifted his arm and also his leg and put them on me. It was the first movement he had made in the hospital. His dad cried and Lisa, Mom and others were amazed. Ben got it in his little box and was very happy. I knew from that time that Caleb and I would be great friends. We loved each other and would play together each day.

A few days later at night Dad and Mom pointed at the light hanging on the wall and said "Colonel, look at you and Caleb." I don't like the noise on the wall and don't often look at the light. It is like other things but doesn't make sense to me. How could things hang on the wall and look smaller than they are?

Alba likes to watch the light when other dogs come on. She talks to them and runs around in circles. Maybe she thinks they will jump down and play with her. Sometimes she offers them one of her bones to make them come down. They never do. Sometimes I think Alba is getting tired. Sometimes she makes big noises with her lungs when she eats dirt. I don't eat dirt, only good treats and apples. Sometimes Dad gives me a piece of a yellow long thing called banana. I like frozen string beans and string cheese... so do Alba and Tanny.

Caleb's visits with Colonel were pivotal in helping motivate him to participate in his difficult physical therapies.

The Howard family's car was hit head-on by a car that had crossed over to the wrong side of the road. Caleb's mom, brother and sister were killed outright. Caleb survived, but suffered a traumatic brain injury and multiple broken bones.

Caleb's Grandmother, Alora Howard (AH): "We didn't have any idea what kind of an experience we were going to have, we didn't even know if he was going to live."

Ben Howard, Caleb's Father (BH): "Early on, before Colonel came, a lot of the progress Caleb was making was so minute that I had become fairly discouraged about his potential for recovery, but when we went into the room with Colonel there was a substantial increase in his awareness. That was a real boost for me— a turning point for me, personally, in my confidence that Caleb had the ability to recover."

AH: "I noticed that every time he would see Colonel, he was more alert, and there was an increase in his awareness.

He'd forget what was "normal" and do just a little bit more than what he had previously been able to accomplish."

Lisa Barnes, Physical Therapist: "To have something much more engaging like Colonel is really helpful. The trick is getting them motivated enough to move, which can be a really hard thing. With an animal, you can immediately see they're much more motivated to try to move, to work on their goals. Colonel did that for Caleb."

BH: "In a hospital, nothing is normal. When an animal comes in, we're no longer in a hospital environment, we're in a play environment ... and the child forgets about therapy and is focused on play. It's absolutely amazing, the effect that the animal therapy has with the children.

"We saw more activity from Caleb when Colonel arrived. Caleb knows it's therapy, it's work and it's going to hurt; when Colonel comes—forget therapy, now it's playtime. That motivates him!"

What therapy animals do best is function as catalysts, helping patients rekindle their desire to heal, to decide that life is worth living, and to get on with the hard work of therapy.

U of U Therapist: "I can't even count the number of my patients who have said, "That's the best therapy, that's the best medicine!" One even said, in my presence, 'Colonel is the best therapist in this hospital!'

Hope can be a medicine, and love can be a cure. Therapy animals are a real medical tool.

Chapter 14

I WOULD LIKE TO tell the story about Ehreth. He was Tim and Karen's dog and was very special, like Yaz. Ehreth got a little bump on his head about the time that Tim got his prize from the big school. Both Ehreth and Tim were graduates like CCI dogs that were special. The bump started to grow and because I have perception I knew it was serious. It stopped some of his eyesight in his left eye and made him have pain. Ehreth never lost his personality and never stopped pulling Tim's wheelchair. He was my hero like my Health Hero prize. I loved Ehreth very much.

During the warm time we went on walks together. I tried to see what I could do to help the bump go down. Sometimes nothing works. It kept growing and soon Ehreth was weaker. Dad went over to Tim's house and a doctor came with a needle to put in Ehreth's foot. It made him fall sleep and go to the Rainbow Bridge. Tim, Karen and Dad cried. We all heard about Ehreth's sleep and felt very sad.

A new dog came. It was after Tim and Karen went on the long ride to CCI in California. They stayed a long time finding a wonderful dog named Sakai. He was black and a Lab. I loved my friend Josh, and hoped Sakai was like him, only black.

Sakai was different. He was raised on a farm with ducks, sheep and chickens. Sakai was very smart. I think that he was the smartest graduate dog since Yazanoff II. The funny thing about Sakai was that he was just like Yaz only slower in his movements and commands. I could tell that Tim and Karen loved Sakai very much.

Tim is slow because he was like Caleb but never got his arms and legs to move. He has been in one of those chairs with wheels for many years. Everyone loves Tim and he is Captain of the Scorpion Quad Rugby team. They go on those noisy air things in the sky to play games in chairs that bump into each other. Tim is a good coach and once played the game. He was very slow and got better at coaching. His team played for the national championship and won. Sakai always goes with Tim even when Dad and Mom take Tim and Karen on a long ride to the real warm place called Hawaii.

Sakai is afraid of water. That is funny for a Lab. But he never was around water except duck ponds. The water in Hawaii is very loud and big waves come in. Sakai told me that he was very afraid the big waves would crash on him. We talk a lot when we are together. He is smarter than me but doesn't get to help as many people. He mostly helps Tim.

Chapter 15

I WANT TO TELL about more of my dog family. Most of my friends have gone to the Rainbow Bridge. Some are still with their families. One that I like is Ben. He is my age and still goes to hospitals. Ben is a yellow Lab and is very brave. He has had surgery. That is when a doctor takes a carving knife and fixes something in your tummy. Ben's mom and dad are Pat and Hank. They live in a big house that has more room to play than my house. I think Ben is very smart.

Tanny is a small golden/yellow lab mix. She lived with us four three years, and then went to a nice home to stay with Madeline. Sharon and Ed also loved her but Madeline really wanted her, and Tanny loved Madeline. I miss Tanny because she was very funny. When she ran, her ears pulled back like running with my Raccoon tied on her head. Tanny has a big yard and a Rottweiler to play with. Rottweilers have a bad image. Sometimes they are mean because their masters want them to be. Most of the time they are very nice. Ed says that Tanny can run faster than their dog the Rottweiler. I am sure she can because she can run faster than any dog.

Tanny at Strawberry Resevoir, flying "on top of the water."

One day Dad took Tanny to his boat and she said she wanted to get in the water. All of the boats were in the water and Tanny thought she could jump off while Dad's boat was going on top of the water fast. Dad tied her to a metal post. Tanny was very upset and Dad knew it. When he came back to the dock he took her to the edge of the water. The only water Tanny had ever seen was when she got her groom. What fun, she thought; I could go on top of that water like the boats.

Dad asked her if she wanted to try, and she did. He unhooked her leash and Tanny ran as fast as she could and jumped from a big rock. She flew in the sky with her ears flopping then hit the water.

Tanny made a big breath and went under. "Why can't I run on top" she said. Her legs started paddling and she came back to Dad. She shook off the water and Dad hooked her up again. The owners of the Strawberry Marina said she was a good swimmer. Dad told her that she was a good swimmer and asked her if she wanted to try again. Tanny said yes.

Her second try was better than the first because Tanny knew that she would go under the water for awhile. She jumped even further and swam around for a while. Tanny never comes when you call her. Finally she came out and ran away. Dad chased her for a long time and finally caught her in the Marina store trying to get food.

I am sure Tanny loves Madeline, but Madeline must be careful when Tanny is around water.

Well, the most important thing happened before Tanny went away. Mom went to CCI and, like me, went for training. She stayed awhile and brought home a little white Lab named Devi. Devi was a facility dog and was trained to go to places to help people. She was trained to be perceptive and learned it very well. Devi must want to go to the hospitals like me.

I hope she likes all of my friends. She is very quiet and reserved when she works. When she plays she is more fun and is a good jumper. Devi is afraid of water like Sakai. Maybe she was raised away from water and never got to jump in it like Tanny. I think my friends at the five hospitals will soon love her. I must teach her many things.

Devi has learned the treat-on-the-nose trick. She can't get the treat every time like I can, but she tries and smiles very big.

She likes apples every night from Dad and likes her butt to be rubbed. She wiggles when anyone rubs it. I love Devi and Mom calls her "Princess Diva." She looks like a princess with a pretty white dress. We need her to dress up for Halloween like a princess. I get in my Darth Vader outfit and scare all of the kids at Halloween time. A guess they aren't really very scared because they know is it just me, the "special boy."

Alba likes Devi because she is a girl. Alba likes to watch the light thing that hangs on the wall and sleep. She loves to go for a short walk but can't run because her back has hurts. Devi wishes she had long fur like Alba. Alba had long fur when she was a puppy.

Alba is my girlfriend even though she takes away my babies and chews the stuffing out of them. I bring them to Dad and he sews them back together. One time Alba went to Dr. Dog and was "Nurse Alba." She wouldn't sit on the chair. Abby was the nurse that day and tried to get her to hold the teddy bears from the children. I am sure the children liked Abby more than Alba, but Alba told me she was very good and the teddy bears had funny smells from the hospital that is why she wouldn't hold them.

Alba is nine and she has a problem that Mom and Dad don't know about. She drinks lots of water and she coughs sometimes. She says that she has the same thing as Florabell. Her lungs are not good from allergies and the dirt she eats.

"Nurse Alba" with Skip and his granddaughter, Abby.

Skip's brother and Colonel's friend, Rod.

Chapter 16

I AM NOW ELEVEN years old and have had a good life. I visited during the cold time four hospitals and made many friends. Devi now comes with Mom and sometimes we go together. Just as the weather was getting real cold, Mom and Dad went to Hawaii again. Some friends met them in Hawaii, including Coach Mike. Mom says he hurt his back while fishing in the big water.

Dad's brother Rod came to stay with us. He has children that also came for awhile. Rod took us on walks each day. He was very nice to us and we love Rod. I think Rod knows about Goldens because he has special love for Alba and me. Alba really likes Rod because Rod takes her on long walks. She never gets to go on longer walks with Mom and Dad. Sometimes her back hurts and sometimes she coughs.

We miss Rod. He has a soft voice like Dad's and we know that he would help us if we needed something.

Dad and Mom came back and brought us some new babies. We are glad they are back and love to be on the bed with them. Now we are back to our normal day and night time.

Sleeps are very important to dogs and we feel safe knowing that Mom and Dad are watching us.

Something is wrong in my tummy. I don't know what it is but it hurts sometimes. I still have my special gift of perception but can't tell Mom and Dad what to do to make me feel better. Maybe it is near my tummy because I can still eat my food and apples without it hurting.

The University Hospital had a special day and invited people to see their new building. I know that it took lots of work to shine up the floors. I walked on the old ones for eight years and they had many bad smells. The dogs were not invited to the special day but got to see what it was all about later. Not only were the floors new but also there were more rooms and better beds. Some of the rooms were for only one person.

Dad put one of his nicest pianos with keys making nice sounds in the first area with new floors. All the people gather around to hear the pretty sounds. I like them, too. They make me feel happy. It reminds me of the time when I played on the keys for a very important man, Roger Williams, at Dad's store. Dad's friend Senator Orrin Hatch was there, and he is friends with Roger. Lots of people were happy then and some dog friends came. Kathy was very happy with the piano and the sounds it made.

Everyone is so nice to me each time I go to work. I love to work and know that I am helping someone feel happy like the piano with nice sounds. I would like to work every day but I feel a little tired now. Maybe one of the nice doctors will tell me about what is wrong with my tummy area. I wish I could be Dr. Dog again and then I could tell myself. Maybe someday I will go to that dog place that has nice doctors just for dogs.

Chapter 17

I FINALLY WENT TO the doctor place and they told me I have a tumor growing near my stomach. I can't jump or it will tear and bleed like Florabell's tumor.

It is spring now, and I love the short walks and my visits to the hospitals. I want to see all of the people I know at each place because Mom tells them about my tumor and that I won't be working any more.

Devi needs to learn lots of things but she may not have time. One time, before my tumor, Mom was trying to get her to jump on a chair. I love to get on chairs. Devi just listened but didn't jump up. She was afraid, so I told her it was OK and the chair was her friend. I jumped up on it then got down so she could see it would be fine. She then jumped up and everyone clapped for her.

No one knows when the pain in my lower stomach area will get really bad and the red stuff will come out. I want to work as long as I can and remember what my mom told me when I was a puppy. Work brings happiness not only to those who I visit but happiness to me. I smile when I am working and feel extra good.

Alba is afraid for me and now shadows me and lies close to me when I am on the floor. She keeps telling me that I will be OK and must keep moving to move my blood supply to the areas that are needed for my heart. She stays up with me at night and sometimes Dad gets up and gives me some water and talks softly to me.

Devi Diva on her rounds at the new Intermountain Medical Center.

Chapter 18

I AM HOME NOW and feel somewhat useless. The doctor lady said I have two months to live at best. Alba feels sad, but I tell her that I will be around longer than she will. She gets mad and tries to make me play with her. Then her brain kicks in and she remembers that if I jump I will break the thin lining separating my tumor and it will bleed. Then I would be in real trouble.

Devi sleeps by me all the day and night. I talk to her about being more engaging. She says she will try but is still very shy. Maybe she just needs practice. Devi looks very graceful when she jumps. She has lots of strength in her legs and back. Getting on a chair should be no problem for her. I am trying to work on her speak. Alba protects the house but we all run out the dog door when a visitor is near our back gate. Most of the time Devi won't bark. I am going to tell her that she must go first and speak to the visitor. After she barks lots of times then Mom can ask her and she will speak.

All dogs require sleep after their food and naps during the day. Our heart rate is faster than humans and we breathe faster.

You see, we are different and don't have long lives and not a lot of time. That is why we have so much love for our masters. We must take advantage of all the time we see them.

I am glad I am Colonel. My life has been very exciting and Dad is writing about it. He reads me different parts and I help him with his words.

Today I chewed up one of my monkeys. It was the one that the nice lady gave me at the University Hospital. I don't usually chew up things but I think I am getting a little bored. Dad has fixed this monkey two times, once after Alba chewed it up and once after I got nervous and chewed off its arms. There are little beads in my monkey and they spill all over the floor. I think Dad put the monkey in a dark box. Tonight I will find my other monkey. It has no beads and smells really good.

Mom says that it will be raining on our run day with Diane. She won't let me run anyway because of my tumor. I hope the day will be better after the rain. I like the smell of the air and how clean my dog run seems. Dad will be home for a little while today because he needs to exercise with Eva. She helps him breathe and makes him stronger. I want Dad to be strong because he must be in charge of all the family. I will be gone soon and will not be able to help him.

Dad will be gone again for a few days. He goes to a city far away in one of those noisy air things and visits with people about pianos. It is funny that he likes pianos because he only plays our piano once in awhile. He sounds sort of bad compared to that man who is called Mr. Piano, Roger Williams. I liked him and he liked me. I don't think he has had a dog friend play the piano before. I surprised him with my two-note paw playing.

Well, I will miss Dad. I promised him not to jump up and tear my tumor loose. I will just take naps and rest. He will call me on that talking thing and I will be happy to hear his voice. I hope he is happy with his visit.

Dad came home to me after three sleeps and was happy, but said "don't jump" to me. I will try to remember better. He gave me my apple and held me close at night. I felt safe and hoped he would not go away again.

Author's Note

Colonel possesses a soul as real as mine. His love is unconditional and will continue throughout this life and the next.

This morning Mom had a call from the nice lady, Lori Tavey, the one who gave me the monkey. She is the Volunteer Program Coordinator for the University Hospital. She said there was a man who needed a liver transplant and got an infection while waiting. He wanted to see a special dog because he was going to die in 24 hours. We went up and I got into bed with him. I knew that he needed me because he had a yellow dog. Maybe Devi would be better because I am a Golden but she is still learning how to perceive people's minds.

This man was waiting for a liver transplant and got an infection. The new liver didn't come, which accelerated his problems. He has some pain, but as he stroked my head some of it went away. I tried very hard to take in his pain but it is more difficult now that I have a tumor and my pain is on and off depending on my movements.

I think Devi will come up also. She is very sweet and may also bring him some love. She had her three-year-old birthday party and is now 21 in people age. That means she is getting smarter each day and no longer a teenager. I love Devi and know she will take my place someday soon. I must teach her to speak and understand the language of eyes.

Today I had a good day even though it has been over a month since my family was told that I only had two months to live. I got a little nervous because Dad was at work and Mom took Devi to do my work at the hospital. She still needs to know how to speak and often misses visiting with people that need her. I chewed up my favorite monkey. Mom had to pick up the insides when she got home with Devi. Alba was embarrassed for me. It's OK because Dad fixed it with that little needle and a string. I love Dad; he fixes things when I mess up.

Chapter 19

I REMEMBER HOW MY tumor started. I went in the morning with Alba for a groom. We went in Dad's car, which is higher than Mom's. I can jump in, but lately it is getting harder. Dad needs to lift Alba in the back with me already there. It didn't take long to get to our groomer's place. We waited in a little fenced off area for our turn.

Mom had a meeting and asked Dad to pick us up. It was just before my food time. I was very excited to get home. I jumped in Dad's car and felt something funny happen in my tummy area. I was sure it would go away, like when I swallow a piece of bone. We got home and I jumped out and Alba jumped just when I did, causing me to go sideways a little. The hurt came back strong. I didn't cry because I thought I needed my food. Alba and I got in the door but I felt real bad and went upstairs to my kennel.

Dad got our food and called to me. I couldn't get out of my kennel and felt very sick. Alba ate her food and Dad came up to see me. It is the first time I missed my afternoon food. It is my favorite time. He lay down by me and talked to me softly.

Dad felt my tummy and it hurt. He stayed by me and brought my water and food up but I didn't eat anything.

Dad stayed long after he should. I know he needed to go to work in his big store. I finally got up and had a little water. Dad fed me some string cheese. It is my favorite treat. A little later I went to bed with Alba and Devi. I knew that Devi would now need to work even harder to learn my job.

The next morning I went to the University Veterinary Clinic. Mom gave me a pill that made me feel a little better that morning, and I wagged my tail a little. I saw a doctor and she looked in all kinds of places then took a picture of my tummy area. Soon I was in a room with Mom and Dad and the doctor. She said that I had a thing around my lower colon called a tumor.

When I jumped out of the car I started the tumor bleeding and lost my energy. I must go in after the next sleep for a CT scan and find out more about the cloud around my lower tummy. My Mom JoLee had one of those things and she is up at Rainbow Bridge waiting for me.

Dad and Mom were very sad, I am eleven years old, which is 77 in people years. I am not tired and last week ran with Mom and Diane. Now I feel a little different.

I always remember when Mom and I go to the Psychiatric Ward at LDS Hospital. It is my favorite place. Everyone loves me there and they are anxious to see me. When I am coming they put a sign in their window. It says, "Colonel is coming today." Another sign says I am on vacation when it is not my day for LDS Hospital. We went there for me to say goodbye to all of my friends. I can't jump up on a chair and must be a little careful about tugs and strenuous activities but we told them that I would only come to visit them.

All of my friends at Psychiatric were sad. I guess that I am sad, too. They really need me to cheer them up and give them the secrets of my perception. You see, I know each of them better than anyone. Their minds speak to me and I can give back. I know that my gift is special. Maybe that is why everyone calls me "special boy."

I was asked to go to the Health Fair at LDS Hospital. The time was Saturday, May 22nd from 11 AM to 2 PM. I know that I have a tumor and was told a month ago that I had two months to live. I feel OK and Mom wants to take me. Dad will come at noon to see if I still have energy to work.

I sat on a chair and shook hands with lots of visitors. Some friends were there and I felt better. Dr. Todd was next to our booth checking eyes. Dad arrived at noon and I felt better. He got me down from the chair and gave me water and asked Mom for cookies. I love cookies and did some of my tricks. There were lots of children that wanted to pet me and hold me. Some visitors had just lost family members or animals and I knew it before they touched me. My friend from the Psych ward was very happy with my work. I went home at 1:30 and took a little nap. I love to do my work and hope I can keep the pain away a little longer.

It is the middle of June now in 2010 and I have almost passed the mark when I am supposed to die. I feel OK but like to sleep a little more than before. Today is another Dr. Dog at Macy's in Tooele. Only Dad and I can go because Mom has other meetings. Last time Alba went and was tired. She told me that Abby was a good nurse but it was very confusing when the Air Med helicopter came. All the papers blew off the tables and people were making noise. There were 300 children lined up outside to see her and she wouldn't hold their teddy bears in her mouth. Alba wanted to lie down and sleep.

It was raining and Dad said we would probably be inside. Macy's had been advertising Dr. Dog for two weeks and even with the rain we might be busy. Sure enough, there were lots of people waiting to see me. The manager of Macy's told Dad that over 400 teddy bears were already gone. I was very tired because I hold each bear in my mouth, tell Dad its problem then shake the child's hand. After a while I decided to get down from the chair and lie down for the rest of the kids. They got down on their knees and looked in my eyes and held their teddy bears by my nose. Some had bad smells. Anyway Dad and I were very tired and drove back to Salt Lake. I took a nap and felt much better. It is fun to go with Dad; he gives me cookies and water and watches me very closely.

It has now been one-and-a-half months since the lady at the Vet place told Mom and Dad that I was going to die. I am feeling OK but not great. I still do some work at LDS Psych unit. I meet with each of my friends and they hold me close. Dad has been giving me more food treats and spends more time talking to me. I want to stay because I love my home and friends. Alba and Devi are afraid for me and everyone gives me extra love.

Mom got a call from a Golden Retriever rescue lady. She said she had some male puppies that needed a home. Mom thought that it was a sign from somewhere and she needed a new puppy. Mom and Dad were convinced to take him. I don't like puppies, especially the one they brought home. His name was Arnie. He holds his tail high and is very aggressive, and also very funny.

Dad has been telling me that Ashley will visit soon with Jay, her father. Ashley was the first girl that I helped in the burn unit of the University Hospital. She was only eight years old and now is 17. Ashley wants to attend the University of Utah. She came to visit me on the 9th of August and I was very glad to see her. She has grown up to be a beautiful girl and very positive and outgoing. She has four dogs like me, two horses and some other animals in Boise. She gave me big loves and Ben came with his box and took pictures of us on chairs while she told her story to the box. The University of Utah thinks that this is a good story. I love Ashley and Jay and they love me. The puppy Arnie was the only bad thing about our meeting. I don't like Arnie very much.

Arnie is now Reggie. His new name is Reginald Daynes at Yale. It sounds like some famous dog but I know he is a monster. He bothers me and I have told him so several times. He cries when I nip him. Dad tells me it is OK. He is now thirteen weeks and has grown an inch a day. Hopefully his brain is growing also. Dad hooks him to his leg because he is bad when he runs free. Poor Devi, she needs to tend him. He thinks he is a stud but Devi, in her sweet way, puts up with his advances.

It has been six weeks since the Vet told Mom and Dad that I was going to Rainbow Bridge. I feel OK most days and go to work once a week at the Psych ward. They love me and I love them. It is now September and I went to the University Health Fair on the 18th. It was a Saturday and Dad could come. Our booth was set up with books for children. It was called "DIVA'S BOOK NOOK." Mom calls Devi "Diva" when she works. Devi was very pleased to have her own booth and lots of helpers to give books. Mom has our paw stamps to put on each book and a small one that says "diva" for the children's wrists.

I was in charge of giving "babies" (small toy animals) to the tiny children in strollers. It was a good job. I was very happy to see so many children friends. Some called me "Doc" because they had seen me as Doctor Dog so many times at University Medical short care centers. After five hours I was getting tired and we went home. The "Diva" booth was a real hit. We had more children with happy parents than any of the other booths. Lori Tavey, Volunteer Program Coordinator for the Hospital, was in charge of the booth. I love Lori, and she loves me.

It is good to be alive these extra months. Dad gives me ice cream and often some of his dinner. He lies by me at night and often gets up to see where I am if I go to my kennel. I know he loves me and helps my headaches. He knows the right place to rub and he holds me when we get on the couch together. Maybe Dad helped me stay longer because before he went fishing at Telegraph Cove in Canada, he gave me a special blessing. I know that soon it will be my time to leave but I don't want to hurt Dad and Mom.

Chapter 20

*W*ELL, SOON I will be going up there to see all of my friends. I know Heavenly Father loves me because He has told me that when I serve others it is the same as serving Him. I will have peace and comfort on my trip. I will miss Mom, Dad, and all of my dog and people friends. I have so many that I want to see them all before I change. Dad's special friend says that I will be blessed for my good works.

My dad is giving a Christmas message in his Church this morning. He says his talk is mostly about me. He will describe how humans need to be perceptive of needs that are within their families. Friend and others outside of their families also need special care. He will emphasize that Christmas is a time of giving love and forgiving. My mother taught me that the big people would often not respond to our love. She said we should keep trying and never give up. It is our role as canine companions to be consistent with our love. My dad will try to help others be consistent with their love to others.

It has been nine months since the doctor told me that I was going to die. Now it is February and I have done several amazing things. Each week I have gone to the psych ward and visited my friends. I still jump up on a chair and get cookies. Maybe I look a little older in my face, but I still feel okay. Some days I have hurts near my tummy and some days I can't eat my food very fast. Dad and Mom give me some of their food. I know that is wrong for a famous therapy dog like me, but it is sure good. I am getting a little fatter.

I think this is the month that Dad and Mom pack those big red bags and go away for lots of sleeps. My dad has loved me more lately and we have been sitting on the couch more while he rubs my ears and holds me.

Uncle Rod, my dad's brother, will be coming to tend Alba and me until Mom and Dad come home. He is very nice and loves us. He will sleep with us and talk to us to keep us from being sad. Alba especially loves Rod. He always takes her for a walk. I go, too. We can't go very far because of our ages, but we check our mail and smell new smells.

I have asked Dad to give me a special blessing before going away. Maybe it will give me some new energy and peace in my mind. I know he will call on that talking thing and Uncle Rod will hold it to my ear. I love to hear Dad's voice. He has the soft voice that I loved when I first came to the big house as a puppy. I need to sleep on a different bed because our normal bedroom is being fixed. Some workers are making lots of noises, and dust is coming down the stairs where Alba and I stay during the afternoon.

Reggie went to see Catherine and she is teaching him lots of things. Catherine is a very nice lady and knows about training puppies. She will take Reggie on walks and he will have fun.

Devi is staying with Amy. Amy and Robert love her and tended her last year. Amy is a CCI puppy-raiser and one of the best. She understands our language. I am sure Devi will have a good time.

It has been almost a year since my visit to the doctor when I was told I would have two months to live. I have been trying hard to help Reggie know that he needs to take care of Dad when I am gone.

Mom and Dad got back from Hawaii and we are all together again. Our house is a mess because there are still workers trying to finish things. I hope everyone can stay home for awhile because I am feeling a little weak and having trouble breathing at night.

Dad had to go to New York again to see about selecting pianos for a large university. I know he didn't want to leave me, but he said he had no choice. He would be gone for only one sleep. He called in the evening when I needed my apple. Mom was tired but gave us our apples.

The next day Dad came home very tired and then needed to go to work. It was okay because I was asked to go to ITA to interview for a PBS show on Channel 11 produced by Cosmic Pictures. The topic is "turning point." Kathy Klotz thought Mom's and my story would be the best one to represent ITA. When I arrived I jumped up on a chair at the conference table. I guess I felt a little pain in my tummy. Kathy gave me some nice cookies that looked like bones wrapped in clear plastic. I held them in my mouth going home in the car because Mom said I couldn't eat them until after my dinner. Alba, Reggie and Devi were waiting for me.

I ate my food, and Mom went upstairs to change her shoes. Something happened in my tummy. I started to cough and I couldn't breathe. My body tightened, and I crouched over and blood came up from my tumors.

Chapter 21

*T*HE COLORS ARE bright and the grass is green. I smell flowers and spring is here sooner than I thought. I see my mother Jo Lee and all of my friends. A big soft voice says, "Well done, my good and faithful servant. You have done it unto the least of my children and loved them ... thus it is as if you have given this love to Me." I feel warm and fresh and must now wait for the rest of my family.

Now I know what perception really is. It is to know how to love everyone and help them every day of my life. I will let you know when it is your turn for my love ... watch for me at the Rainbow Bridge.

With special love,

COLONEL

Colonel Daynes died on March 11, 2011, at 3:45 pm. His body was taken to University Pet Clinic and prepared. Many, many letters and flowers, as well as stories on live and printed media, have appeared since this day. His marvelous perception predicted that he would cause any more anxiety to his family by taking time to leave this earth. He went fast, and just after an interview which could be a "turning point" for someone reading his story.

Thanks to Susan for taking Colonel to the hospitals and sharing his love with each new friend. Thanks also to Kathy Klotz, Executive Director of Intermountain Therapy Animals, for helping me assemble this unique story of Colonel.

—*Skip Daynes*

Susan and Colonel (portrait by Ben Cook)

Kathy and Emily

. . . .

Colonel Daynes

March 28, 1999 — March 11, 2011

On Friday afternoon, March 11, Colonel, Golden Retriever Partner of Skip and Susan Daynes of Salt Lake, went to the Rainbow Bridge. He would have been 12 on March 28th.

Susan had to go out of town Saturday morning, and she asked me to let you all know, since so many have known them and expressed concern over Colonel's ongoing bout with cancer.

Susan and Colonel worked together for almost ten years, first joining ITA as pet partners in May of 2001. Colonel was raised by Susan as a potential service dog for Canines Companions for Independence, but he did not graduate as a service dog because he was "too social," so he came back to Susan. While she was initially disappointed, she soon realized that his true calling was always to be a therapy animal and that the career change was simply meant to be.

Colonel was chosen ITA's Therapy Animal of the Year in 2003, and received the inaugural "Ginjer AAT Award" in 2005. He was honored by the University of Utah, and chosen as a Utah Healthcare Hero. He starred in lots of newspaper and magazine articles, and TV and video productions. We were fortunate to be the organization that Colonel represented, and there are literally thousands of people who were touched by his doggy medicine.

But the numbers and facts don't really convey the essence. Clearly, Colonel was a dog who had a mission, and he lived it thoroughly and wholeheartedly throughout his life, giving and receiving love to the max. There are a thousand stories from all those clients. One classic came from an ex-military observer, after watching what Colonel did for his wife in a physical therapy session. He told Susan that Colonel should be promoted to a Five-Star General.

Colonel was diagnosed with hemangiosarcoma on April 21, 2010. His vets told Susan and Skip that he would live for no more than two months at the outside, so they elected not to do any chemotherapy, as the tumor was inoperable. But he had more to live for, obviously, because he continued to do his therapy work for almost 11 more months.

In fact, he lived to the fullest up to and including his last afternoon, which he spent at the ITA office, treating the staff, our guests, and even our postlady to his attention and affection. He came joyfully in, as was his habit, and jumped into a chair at the conference table. He also jumped into the front passenger seat of Susan's SUV when the meeting was over two hours later, holding a cellophane bag of treats in his mouth all the way home.

When they arrived home, Susan fed the dogs their dinner. Colonel ate with his usual relish. She went upstairs to change her shoes and returned just five minutes later to find Colonel's body on the floor. He was gone.

The shock was almost too much after the fun afternoon we had all spent. But as I think on it, I find a sense of wonder in the way he departed earth. We should all be so lucky, to live a life full to the last moment, and then leave in a flash. The shock and suddenness are tough on the loved ones left behind, but it's a blessing not to have to make the grievous decision to end the life of a companion you love, or to watch helplessly as the quality of their lives deteriorates.

Colonel was an inspiring and exemplary therapy dog, and there will be legions of us who will miss him. Our hearts are with Susan and Skip.

—*Kathy Klotz*

Dear Susan & Skip,

I was so sorry to learn of Colonel's recent passing. What an amazing friend he was to you and countless others! He became such an important part of our Hannah's recovery and our family story—just like he did for other children and adults.

We credit Colonel with bringing Hannah out of her coma and into an awareness of her surroundings so she could take an active role in her own recovery. She often tells people, "Colonel burped and I woke up."

Without your loving training and management of Colonel, we would never have had this therapeutic help in Hannahs's life. We cannot thank you adequately for your role.

Colonel's gentle life will shine on in the lives of so many children, adults and families. We will never forget him or you.

Julie Landeen
Hannah Sessions' grandmother

P.S. Hannah is now in 7th grade and continues to learn and improve every day. She is enrolled in regular classes with some support from special education. She brings us joy every day. And she now volunteers at the Humane Society animal shelter!

Caleb and Hannah with Colonel, playing at the park during filming of their TV story.

Colonel the Golden Retriever

Pet Partner® with Susan Daynes
Members of Intermountain Therapy Animals
in Salt Lake City

*S*USAN SAYS OF Colonel, "He knows his job. When he puts on his red scarf he is ready to work and his demeanor changes. He is so intuitive and always knows what a person needs. Every time we start in a new place, he figures out quickly how to make a difference and touch lives. He takes over and makes magic.

"I was fortunate to watch when he worked with 9-year-old Ashley in the burn unit; I saw him comfort her when she was undergoing her therapy and was in extreme pain. He would gently put his paw on her hand. We watched her reach her goal of walking for the first time, taking Colonel around the unit.

I watched his brain-injured client speak for the first time, saying 'Come on, boy,' and of course Colonel obliged. I've watched him when he is helping his clients work on strength and balance by playing tug. He always knows just how hard to pull, based on how strong or weak his client is.

"He will keep up retrieving forever, whether the ball just trickles slightly or flies down the hall. Colonel happily brings it back as many times as they want. I've watched him comfort those who are sad. He stays close and quiet while the tears flow.

"Children love him. We have worked with three girls at Primary Children's Residential Treatment Center. Each one has had different needs, but Colonel knows how to work his way into each heart. Our first client had trouble forming relationships, and when we first met she preferred to talk to a lamp or a computer rather than Colonel. But Colonel, master that he is, won her over. They spent  hours playing. She would throw his ball and then say, 'Squeak it!' and he would comply, every time, making her laugh and laugh. When she left, she kissed Colonel on the head and told him, "I love you"—she had come a long way from talking to a lamp!

"One of Colonel's clients said, right in front of his speech, physical and occupational therapists, 'Colonel is the best therapist that works at this hospital!' His therapists laughed appreciatively! And the husband of one client told me, after watching her session, 'Colonel should be promoted to Five-Star General!'

Susan and Colonel work with Connor McCloy, a young man who is just graduating from his wheelchair. Colonel loves to ride in wheelchairs, and his clients love to "return the favor" after they have regained the strength and skill to do so. Such an activity has emotional and psychological therapeutic benefits for the patients, but everyone involved finds it rewarding.

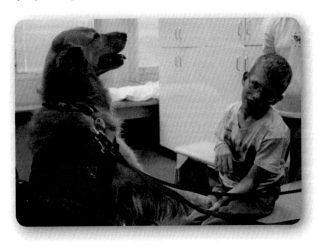

"I've seen Colonel give love to every human being he comes in contact with. It doesn't matter if they are sick and hooked to machines and tubes. He finds a way to get as close as he can and shows his love and concern.

Colonel with two other of his clients at the Primary Children's facilities.

Dennis Moore wanted closeness and a kiss. Colonel will assume any position that a patient desires, and he offers kisses as gently as a whisper.

I would like to give you my perspective on how Colonel has helped my husband's rehab.

On June 4, 2006, my husband Dennis Moore fell from the roof of our house. It was his 55th birthday. In one instant Dennis came near to death, injured his spinal cord and fractured his C1 and C2 vertebrae. He was not expected to live through the night. We spent 42 days in the ICU in Billings and then transferred to Salt Lake City University Hospital for extensive rehab.

The first real smiles of joy came across my husband's face the day he met Colonel. A beautiful and gentle golden retriever not only reminded us of home, but also took this clinical experience away, if only for a short time. Colonel and his owner Susan Daynes have really been a sight for sore eyes. Dennis looks forward to Thursdays and his visits with Colonel. Colonel's unconditional love, gentle nature and healing therapies have made Dennis' stay endurable. In the photo, Dennis wanted Colonel's closeness and a kiss. Colonel was as gentle as a whisper. We miss home and family, but can tolerate the separation knowing that caring people in the hospital will make our stay as pleasant as possible. Colonel is truly a part of Dennis' treatment team. He's an awesome friend.

Vicki Moore
311 Clark Avenue, Billings, MT 59101, 406-259-0700

. . . .

. . . .

My name is Johnathn Stovall
and to meet Colonel was a blast
because it made me feel happy and
at home. He also made me laugh.
I hope to see him the next time I
come in to the hospital. I feel that
he desirves this award for that reason.

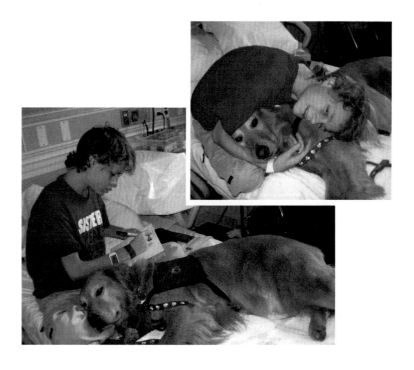

. . . .

Susan and Colonel Elected to TTA Hall of Fame in 2007

S USAN HAS BEEN an exemplary volunteer in all possible aspects and dimensions. Scarcely an issue goes by that you don't hear of something more they have been doing. In delivering our front-line services to clients, she and Colonel have no peers, in either quality or quantity. In doing all the extras, she always gives 110%. Whether serving on the board, raising funds, chairing committees, serving as a Team Evaluator, mentoring others, or finding us new friends, contacts and public attention, Susan is always there. Here's what she says:

"As most of you already know, I have been a member of Intermountain Therapy Animals (ITA) for some 8 years now. I am blessed to volunteer with my beloved Colonel, a truly inspirational therapy dog. Most recently he has been featured in an article in *PARENTS* magazine (September 2008), in an upcoming documentary film called, "Sit. Stay. Heal," and has been honored as a Utah Healthcare Hero by the University of Utah (the first dog to be so recognized among physicians and other professionals).

"Awards are great, but our true rewards come from being there for each magical moment when Colonel makes a significant difference for someone who is struggling to heal: Hannah, the 8-year-old near-drowning patient who uttered her first sound—a giggle, when she heard Colonel burp; John, the man who grinned after quadruple bypass surgery when he saw Colonel—and his wife, who said, 'There was so much life pouring into my husband because of the presence of that healing dog;' Ashley, the little girl in the Burn ICU trying to deal with painful therapies after being hit by a car and dragged beneath it. The list goes on. One stroke patient's husband, watching Colonel help her with her rehab therapies, declared, 'Colonel? He should be promoted to 5-star general!'"

Thank you, Susan, and welcome to the ITA Hall of Fame!

• •

THE HYDRANT

March 2005

THE MONTHLY BULLETIN FOR INTERMOUNTAIN THERAPY ANIMALS' VOLUNTEERS
VOL. XII / NO.3

Colonel (Daynes) Wins Inaugural 2004 Ginjer Award

The very first ITA "Ginjer Award" for outstanding service in AAT was awarded to Colonel, Pet Partner® of Susan Daynes of Salt Lake, at the Volunteer Celebration on February 15, 2005.

Colonel the Golden Retriever has been an ITA therapist for more than three years now. He works in many settings, including Rehab at LDS Hospital, the Burn Unit at University

Hospital, Primary Children's Residential Treatment Center, and the Bennion Elementary R.E.A.D. Program, as well as appearing at countless ITA school and community presentations.

Susan says of Colonel, "He knows his job. When he puts on his red scarf he is ready to work and his demeanor changes. He has an innate sense and seems to always know what a person needs. Every time we start in a new place, he figures out quickly how to make a difference and touch lives. He takes over and makes magic.

"I was fortunate to be there when he worked with his 9-year-old girl in the burn unit; I saw him comfort her when she was undergoing her therapy and was in extreme pain. He would gently put his paw on her hand. I was there when she reached her goal of walking for the first time, taking Colonel for a walk around the unit.... I was there when his brain-injured client spoke for the first time, saying 'Come on, boy,' and of course Colonel ran right to him. I've watched him when he is helping his clients work on strength and balance by playing tug. He always knows just how hard to pull, based on how strong or weak his client is.

"I am there when he retrieves. He will keep it up forever, whether the ball just trickles slightly or flies down the hall, Colonel happily brings it back as many times as they want.... I've been there when he comforts someone who is sad. He stays closed while the tears flow.

"Children love him. We have worked with three girls at Primary RTC. Each one has had different needs, but Colonel knows how to work his way into each heart. Our first client had trouble forming relationships, and when we first met she preferred to talk to a lamp or a computer rather than Colonel. But Colonel, master that he is, won her over. They spent hours playing. She would throw his ball and then say, 'Squeak it!' and he would comply, every time, making her laugh and laugh. When she left, she kissed Colonel on the head and told him, "I love you"—a long way from talking to a lamp!

"The therapists are touched as well. I was there when one of his clients said, right in front of his speech, physical and occupational therapists, 'Colonel is the best therapist that works at this hospital!' I was also there when the husband of our client told me, 'Colonel should be promoted to 5-Star General!'

"I've seen Colonel give love to every human being he comes in contact with. It doesn't matter if they are sick and hooked to machines and tubes. He finds a way to get as close as he can and shows his love and concern.

"I truly think Colonel was destined to be a therapy dog. I am so glad to have found ITA and to have the opportunity to visit so many places. I believe I have been given a gift to raise such a wonderful animal and am grateful I can share him with others."

Here are some selected comments from the many therapists and clients who wrote to support Colonel's nomination:

Colonel Wins 2005 Ginjer Award

Colonel's visits are a welcome change of pace for patients here on the LDS Rehab unit. All his activities help us challenge patients' balance and motor control and also help us engage them in what are otherwise mundane therapeutic exercises. Colonel's warm eyes and spirit, and his endless desire to interact with patients, make him an ideal therapy dog whose visits are highly anticipated by patients and therapists alike. As a matter of fact, most patients swear he is smiling at them! We are very grateful to Colonel and Susan for their dedication and consistency in serving patients.

—Lance Willingham, P.T. LDS Rehab Unit

Colonel – Wonder Dog! The University has truly been blessed by the many hours of service from Colonel Daynes. The moment he arrives, we know that he is ready to work, happy, well-behaved and wagging his tail. He has this keen sense of patients' needs. He is very sensitive and very talented. He speaks in four languages, and he has the skill to know when to let go with a bark or a quiet whimper. He can detect the need for affection and comfort, and will freely give it. His talents are used to help people talk, walk and remember again. When he walks into the room, he brings "home," "love," and disengagement from the hospital to his clients. Colonel is the best therapy that could happen to patients, their family, and our staff.

—Shauna Smith, R.T.
University of Utah Hospital Rehab Unit

Colonel and Susan have become an integral part of our treatment and have shown an amazing capacity to form positive connections with not only the child they have been assigned to, but to every child on the unit. At times they have been the primary support for children who have no other family to provide this support while they are in treatment.

Colonel seems to have an innate sense that helps him relate to even the most difficult children. He is very gentle and allows each child to make the connections they are comfortable with, when they are ready. Much of his best work is done when he is simply sitting close, with his head and paw on a child's lap, while the child talks with him, brushes his coat or pets him. In these moments he is able to do something that many people are not able to do—form relationships that these children feel safe and comfortable in, and that is amazing!

—Carie Carter, Therapist
Primary Children's RTC

Colonel contributes a lot of love and affection to me. He is there for me always. We have made a lot of good memories, including going on walks, meeting my sister, Christmas and birthday parties. I feel really cared for and loved when I see Colonel. When he doesn't come, I miss him a lot and wish he was here to comfort me. He is always there in my heart when I am sad. Colonel always comes to cheer for me when I have been in music or dance programs. He has been here for all the special times in my life, and makes me feel special when he is here. Because he loves me so, it is easy for me to love him back. He is my best friend. No other dog or person could take his place.

—Child at Primary Children's RTC

We hope many of you will be inspired by Colonel's example to try your paws at delving deeper into the powerful potential of assisting clients with their therapeutic goals. We have several facilities in which this kind of work is done and they are looking for additional teams. Please contact Karen Burns or Kathy Klotz for more information.

—Kathy Klotz

Colonel smiles with one of his rehab clients at LDS Hospital.

Colonel and Skip in the Deseret News

Deseret Morning News

EDUCATIC

MARY FINCH, EDUCATION EDITOR, 237-2140

Erik Ritter, a sixth-grader at Longview Elementary, has some fun with with Colonel, a golden retriever. READ dogs offer a warm heart and a wet nose to students practicing their reading skills.

Readin

goes to the dogs

By Jennifer Toomer-Cook and Tiffany Erickson
Deseret Morning News

Angels and hearts—common themes in my volunteer work with Colonel, my therapy dog. Chico's helps me dress the part, but for Colonel it's intrinsic. He's a motivator without peer in the Burn ICU and Rehabilitation. One patient said, "He's the best therapist in this hospital!" Another: "Colonel should be promoted to Five-Star General!" He happily does whatever his clients need, from playing tug with a stroke patient to baking cookies with a child. He inspired one comatose little girl to wake with a giggle when he burped. Everyone he meets feels loved. Dogs know that's what it's all about.

—Susan Daynes
Salt Lake City, Utah

Special Report - Best Hospitals

COMFORT. Susan Baynes and Colonel help with pet therapy at the University of Utah Hospital.

RETIREES ARE ENJOYING ACTIVE LIFESTYLES, WHICH MEANS FEWER HOURS TO VOLUNTEER.

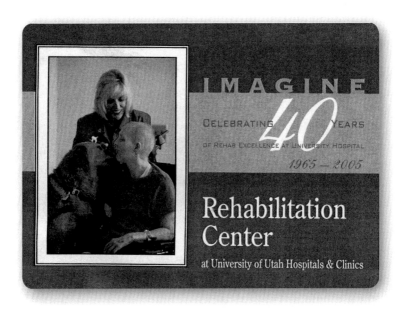

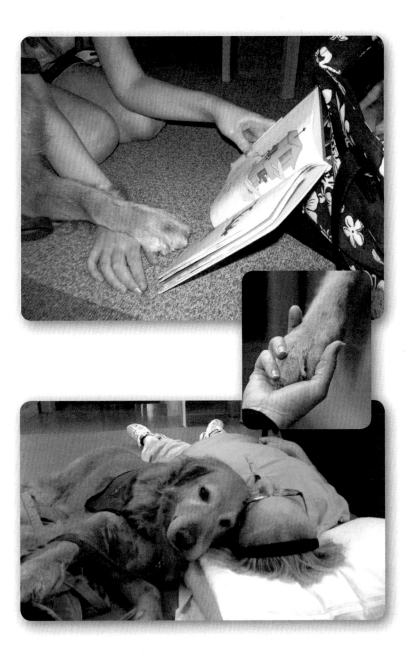

(ABOVE:) *Tim with seven of his best friends, wishing his mom a Happy Mother's Day: (from left) Flora, Alba, Dutchie, Colonel, Ehreth, Gia and Max. (BELOW:) Tim's newest partner, Sakai, enjoying the beach in Hawaii.*

If you would like to see Colonel in action, bringing hope, joy and healing to many of his patient-clients, a DVD is available for a $20 donation to Intermountain Therapy Animals.

Please call 801-272-3439 to request a copy.

82890498R00073

Made in the USA
San Bernardino, CA
20 July 2018